CASTLE IRVINE, IRVINESTOWN, IRELAND

THE IRVINES

AND THEIR KIN.

A History of the Irvine Family and Their Descendants.

COMPILED AND EDITED BY

Mrs L. Boyd

Louisville Ky
Printed for the Author,

TABLE OF CONTENTS.

PREFACE.

T HE author is indebted to Rev Dr Christopher Irvine, of Mountjoy, Ireland,
Sir Wm D'Arcy Irvine, Irvine Castle, Ireland, Mr Andrew M Sea, Louisville, Ky,
Col R. T Irvine, Big Stone Gap, Va, and
Mr James Callaway, of Macon, Ga, for
material assistance in writing this book.
She commends it, with its faults and inaccuracies, which are all her own, to the
charitable criticism of her kinsfolk.

L BOYD

DUM MEMOR IPSE MEI

Irvine.

THE IRVINES OR IRWINS OR IRVINGS

OF THE

OLD COUNTRY AND THE NEW.

The Scottish Irvines.

"There were two branches of the Irvine family that belonged to the baronage — Bonshaw and Drum. The Lairds of Drum were descended from William de Irvine, who was armor-bearer to Robert Bruce, and was rewarded for his devoted services by a giant of the forest of Drum, Aberdeenshire, at that time part of a royal forest "

Sir Alexander Irvine, grandson of William de Irvine, was one of the chief commanders of the king's army at the battle of Harlaw, A D 1411 He was a valiant champion In a hand-to-hand encounter with Eachin Ruadh mir Cath, of Clan McLean of Dowart, general of Donald of the Isles, "they fought like lions and killed one another dead on the spot." The prowess of this gude Sir Alexander Irvine is especially celebrated in the battle of Harlaw Other heads of the family rendered important services to subsequent sovereigns, and in the seventeenth century the Lands of Drum vied in wealth and power with many families of noble rank

Sir Alexander Irvine, the Royalist, was eldest son of Alexander, ninth Laird of Drum, by Lady Marian, daughter of Robert Douglas, Earl of Buchan He was born about 1598, and died May, 1658 He had a varied and stirring life He was one of Charles II's most earnest Scottish supporters, and when Charles became king, in 1660, he offered Sir Alexander's son Alexander, tenth Laird of Drum, an earldom, which was refused Sir Alexander, the Royalist, after the reverses his party suffered, was led to conform to the Covenant, though unwillingly, and was appointed sheriff of Aberdeen in December, 1634 By his wife, Magdalen, daughter of Sir J. Scrymgeour, he had, besides other children, two sons Alexander, who died 1687 (spoken of above), and Robert, who died February 6 1645, in the tolbooth of Edinburgh (see "Memorials of the Trouble," Spalding Club, Gordon's "Scots Affairs," Spalding Club, "Miscellany of Spalding Club," Vol 3, "Burk's Landed Gentry," and "Dictionary of National Biography," Stephens)

Christopher Irvine, M D, who flourished between 1638 and 1685 — phy-

sician, philologist and antiquary — was a younger son of Christopher Irvine, of
Robgill Tower, Anandale, and a barrister of the Temple, of the family of
Irvine of Bonshaw, in Dumfriesshire   He calls himself on one of the title
pages "Irwinus abs Bon Bosco"   He was a brother of Sir Gerard Irvine,
Bart , of Castle Irvine, of Fermanaugh, who died at Dundalk, 1689   Christo-
pher was a Royalist and an Episcopalian   He says that he was historiographer
to Charles II   He married Margaret, daughter of James Wishard, Laird of
Potterow, and had two sons   Christopher, M D , and James   This Christo-
pher died about 1685.   He wrote many books, and his principal ones are (1)
"Bellum Grammaticale," Edin , 1650, 1658, and again 1698 . (2) " Medicina
Magnetica, or the Arts of Curing by Sympathy," London, 1656 , (3) "Index
Locorum Scotorum," Edin , 1664 ["An useful piece, and well deserves a new
impression "— By Nicholson's "Scot Hist Lib '], (4) "Histori Scoticae,
Nomenclature Latino Vernacula," 1682, 1692, again 1819   (See Chambers'
"Dictionary of Eminent Scotsmen," and " Burk's Landed Gentry ")

The following account of the Irvines is compiled from Robert Doglas'
" Baronage of Scotland " and " Peerage of Scotland ".

ELIZABETH, daughter of Sir Robert Keith (who was alive in 1421), heiress
of Troup, married to Alexander Irvine, of Drum

ELIZABETH, daughter of William, fourth Earl Marischal (who died October
7, 1581), by his wife, Margaret married to Sir Alexander Irvine, of
Drum.

ISABEL, daughter of Sir Robert Campbell, Glenurchy (who succeeded his
brother 164–), by Isabel, daughter of Lachlan Macintosh, Captain Clan-
chattan, married to Robert Irvine, of Fedderet, son of Alexander Irvine,
of Drum, and had two daughters.

MARGARET, daughter of John Johnston, of Johnston, Marquis of Anandale,
married to Christopher, son and heir of Edmond Irvine, of Bonshaw,
in the county of Dumfries— contract dated 1566

ELIZABETH, third daughter of Sir Alexander, Lord Forbes (son of Sir
John — died 1405), by Lady Elizabeth Douglas (daughter of George,
Earl of Angus, and granddaughter of King Robert II — 1371–1390),
married to Irvine, of Drum.

SIR ARCHIBALD DOUGLAS (son of Sir William, who fell at Flodden,
1513), of Glenbowie, was knighted by James V (1513–1542) , married
(1) Agnes Keith, daughter of William, Earl of Marischal, and had one
son and one daughter , married (2) Mary, daughter of Sir Alexander
Irvine, of Drum, and had issue (see below)

LADY JANET, daughter of Robert Douglas, Earl of Buchan, by Christina
(daughter died 1580), widow of Richard Douglas, married to Alexander
Irvine, of Drum

MARY, daughter of George Gordon, second Marquis Huntley (who was
beh ·l l a Ma' (C   Edinburgh March ·   1649 ' by Lady Jane

Campbell, eldest daughter of Archibald, seventh Earl Argyll (died June 14, 1638) married to Alexander Irvine, of Drum, December 7, 1643

SIR ARCHIBALD DOUGLAS, by marriage with Mary Irvine, daughter of the Laird of Drum had two sons—James and John—and six daughters—Isabel, Sarah, Margary, Eupham and Grizel Margary, fourth daughter, married to Irvine, of Ballie

SIR WILLIAM DOUGLAS (living in 1635), great grandson of Sir Archibald, married a daughter of Alexander Irvine, of Drum, by whom he had one son — Sir William, his successor

WILLIAM LESLIE, fourth Baron of Balquhair (who died in the reign of James III, 1467), by Dame Agnes Irvine, his second wife, a daughter of the Laird of Drum, had a son, Alexander, who was the progenitor of the Leslies of Waldis

JAMES CRICHTON, Viscount of Frendraught, married (2), at the church of Drumoak, November 8, 1642 Margaret, daughter of Sir Alexander Irvine, of Drum and had two sons — James, second Viscount of Frendraught, and Lewis, third Viscount of Frendraught

SIR GEORGE OGILVY married (1) Margaret, daughter of Sir Alexander Irvine, of Drum, and had one daughter — Helen, who married Earl of Airly Sir George, of Dunlugus, had a charter to himself and Margaret Irvine, his wife, of the barony of Dunlugus (March 9, 1610-11), and another barony of Inschedrour, wherein he is designated "younger Banff" (February 14, 1628) Died August 11, 1663

JAMES OGILVY (fifth Baron of Boyne, died 1619), had one son, Walter, his successor. James' charter dated February 22, 1597 Jacabo Ogilvy, apparenti de Boyne, et Elizabeth Irvine ejus spousae, terrarum de Quhinter, Cavintoun, Kindrocht, et dimedietet terraum de Ardbragane

NORMAN LEITH, successor to Laurence Leith his father (who died in the reign of James III, 1460–1488), married Elizabeth daughter of William Leslie, fourth Baron Balquhair, by Agnes Irvine, his wife, daughter of a Baron of Drum Norman died during the reign of James III

SIR JOHN OGILVIE, of Innercarity (who was, by Charles I, created Baronet of Nova Scotia in 1626), married Anne, daughter of Sir Alexander Irvine, of Drum, issue, four sons and one daughter

ALEXANDER SEION, of Meldrum, in his father's lifetime, got a charter under the great seal, dated 1578, for lands of Meldrum He married (1) Elizabeth, daughter of Sir Alexander Irvine, of Drum — then only son, Alexander, died in 1590, during his father's lifetime, married (2) Jean, daughter of Alexander, Lord Abernethy John Urquhart, who died November 8, 1631 (at 84), and was succeeded by his son, John (died December, 1631), got a charter, under the great seal, upon his father's resignation — Johannes Urquhart, Juniori, de Craigfintry, et Isabella Irvine, ejus spousae — of the lands of Leathers and Craigfintry, in

2

Aberdeenshire, dated July 28, 1612. By his first wife, Isabella, he had a son, John

JEAN first daughter of Sir John Johnston, sheriff of Aberdeen (1630), married to Irvine of Brakely

THOMAS JOHNSTON, eldest son of John Johnston, of that ilk married (1) Mary, daughter of Irvine, of Kingouffie They had four sons — Thomas (died in 1656), William, John and James — and three daughters

A daughter of Patrick Forbes, of Caise, was married, in the sixteenth century, to Irvine, of Bettie

GEORGE, second son of George Dundas, of that ilk, had a daughter Barbara to marry Alexander Irvine, of Supack, or Saphock, in the seventeenth century

ELIZABETH, daughter of Alexander Seton, of Pitmedden (who died soon after, in 1630), married Patrick Irvine, of Beatty

MARY, daughter of Jenet and William Johnston, Esq., married to James Irvine, of Cove, in the latter part of the seventeenth century

JANET, second daughter of Sir John Douglas, of Kelhead (son of Sir William), married at Prestonfield, November 13, 1767, to William Irvine, of Bonshaw , they had one son and one daughter

HON EMILIA ROLLO, daughter of Andrew, third Lord Rollo (died in March, 1700), by Margaret Balfour (died October 20, 1734) — Andrew and Margaret married November 1670 — married to William Irvine, of Bonshaw, in the county of Dumfries. September 2, 1698, and died, his widow, at Bonshaw, March 20, 1747 (æt 71)

HON CLEMENT ROLLO (fourth son of Robert, fourth Lord Rollo, who died April 16, 1765, aged eighty), who died at Duncrumb, January 14, 1762, married Mary Emilia, eldest daughter of John Irvine, of Bonshaw, and had issue Robert, a captain in Forty-second Regiment Foot, who settled in America 1784 , John, barrackmaster at Perth . and Mary, who died at Perth October 12, 1776

MARGARET, daughter of Alexander Skene, of that ilk, who succeeded his father, James Skene, 1612, married to Robert Irvine, of Fornet, and Monteoffe

JOHN CAMPBELL (son Hon John Campbell), member of parliament for the boroughs of Ayr, 1796, 1802 and 1806, married (1) a daughter of Mr Peter, merchant in London, widow of —— Irvine, by whom he had a daughter, Caroline

ALEXANDER IRVINE, of Coul, was a witness to a charter, dated August 8, 1539, to John Keith, of Craig who succeeded John Keith, proprietor of barony of Craig

The Irvines as Men of Letters.

Alexander Irvine "De Jure Regni Diascepsis ad Regem Carolum," Ludg , Bat , 1627

Rev Alexander Irvine "Cause and Effect of Emigration from the Highlands, ' 1802, noticed by Sidney Smith in ' Edinburgh Review '

Alexander Irvine "London Flora, ' London, 1838 and 1846

Alexander Forbes Irvine "Prae-Treatise on the Game Laws of Scotland," 1850. Edin ["The latest, fullest, and most complete collection of the forest laws, and the rules of game in bird and beast "—Perth Courier]

Andrew Irvine "Sermons," 1830 ["Good specimens of sound reasoning, pure theology and practical applications "—London, Christian Reerumb]

William Irvine, M D (1) "Essays on Chemical Subjects " edited by his son, W J M D , London, 1805 (2) "Theories of Heat," Nic Jour , 1803 See same in 1805

William Irvine, M D , son of preceeding William (1) "On Disease," 1802, (2) "Letters on Sicily," 1813 , (3) "Latent Heat," Nic. Jour , 1804

Patrick Irvine (1) "Considerations on the Inexpediency of the Law of Entail in Scotland," second edition, Edin 1826 ["A very short and very sensible book, on a subject of the utmost importance to Scotland "—Edin Review, No 36 "An ably written and philosophical tract in opposition to the practice of entail "—McCulloch Lit of Polit Econ] (2) "Considerations on the Independency of the Law of Marriage in Scotland, ' 1828 ["Much valuable matter collected from many authentic sources ' —Law Chronicle]

Ralph Irvine (1) "Peruvian Bark," Edin , 1785 , (2) "Dispensations," 1786

It may be seen, by referring to "Burk's General Armory," that Irvine (Arlingford, Scotland) has arms A1 —three holly branches, each consisting of as many leaves, ppr , banded gules, within a bordure, indented, vert Crest—two holly leaves in saltire, vert Motto — Sub sole vinesco Irvine (Drum, county Aberdeen), descended from William de Irwin, whom Robert Bruce, his armor bearer, etc Ar —three small shafts or bunches of holly, two and one vert, each consisting of as many leaves slipped of the last, banded gules Crest—a sheaf of nine holly leaves Supporters, two savages wreathed about the head and middle with holly, each carrying in his hand a baton ppr Motto — Sub sole, sub umbra virens

Irvine (Castle Irvine, county Fermanaugh, Baronet, descended from the Irvines of Bonshaw Of the Irish branch was Sir Gerard Irvine, created a baronet (29) by Charles II His present representative is Sir Gorges Marcus d'Arcey-Irvine, of Castle Irvine, Baronet, son and heir of William Mervyn Irvine, Esr , of Col Irvine by his widow, re the late of Gorges Lowther,

Esq , of Kilune, County Meath, member of parliament, and grandson
of Christopher Irvine, Esq , of Castle Irvine, by Mary, his wife, second
daughter and coheir of Sir Audley Mervyn, of Trillick Castle, County Tyrone,
Kut) Ar —a fess gules between three holly leaves, ppr   Crest—A dexter
arm in armor fessways, issuant out of a cloud, a hand ppr holding a
thistle, also ppr   Motto—Dum memor ipse mei

In the coats of arms of the Irvines, Irvins, Irvings and Irwins holly
leaves or the thistle are always to be found — one or both

The American Irvines.

The American Irvines are of Scotch descent, being descended in a direct
and unbroken line from the ancient house of Bonshaw, Scotland.

Robert Irvine fled from Scotland to Gleno, Ireland, in 1584   He married
Elizabeth Wylie, and they had one son, David, who married Sophia Gault,
whose family were of the nobility of Scotland, and descended from the Shaws,
who built Ballygally Castle on the shore of Larne in 1625. Above the en-
trance door of this castle is this inscription. "God's Providence is my inheri-
tance." Previous to the time of their building Ballygally Castle on the shore
of Larne, they had been Lairds of Greenock in Scotland   The Shaws intermarried with the Bissets.

The following was sent me from Larne, Ireland

" The ruins of Olderfleet Castle, near Larne Harbor — the original size of
this castle was considerably larger than it appears at present, and there is good
reason for fixing the period of its erection at or about the year 1242, by a
Scotch family by the name of Bisset, who were compelled to leave Scotland,
owing to their implication in the murder of Patrick Comyn, Earl of Athol.
The castle was at one time important as a defensive fortress against the preda-
tory bands of Scotch who infested the northeastern coast, and once under
the direction of a governor   The office was held in 1569, by Sir Moyses Hill,
but in 1598 it was thought no longer necessary and accordingly abolished
The castle and adjoining territory were granted in 1610, to Sir Arthur Chi-
chester, the founder of the noble family of Donegal   It was here that Edward
Bruce, the last monarch of Ireland, landed with his band of Scotch, when he
endeavored to free Ireland from English rule in 1315 "

The son of David Irvine and Sophia Gault — James — married Margaret
Wylie, and had ten children born to him, viz   Margaret, who married her
cousin, Ephraim McDowell , Mary, who married her cousin, John Wylie (both
Mary and Margaret died in Ireland. and he buried in the old churchyard of
Raloo) T   .   h   .   .—— and settled at Cushendal, Ireland,
where he lived and died and where his descendants now reside , Alexander,

AULT ARMS

MOTTO: Laudem implebitur

who married a kinswoman, a Miss Gault, George, David, William, Robert, James and Samuel .

The seven last named Irvines all came to America between the years of 1725 and 1731   Alexander Irvine lived in Scotland, and he and his brother, Robert, were at a hunt in Argyleshire, where Alexander got into a difficulty with a man and gave him wounds from which he died   He and Robert fled from Scotland, in hunting dress, and came, by night, to Gleno   Alexander was afterwards pardoned for his offense and returned to Scotland, and came from there to America, landed at Philadelphia, and went from there to Bedford county, Va

This is the tradition that goes lamely about Gleno to this day

While Alexander Irvine was at Gleno he fell in love with a beautiful Irish girl, of low degree, and she returned his love   They were in the habit of meeting at the Irvine and MacDowell mill at night-fall, beneath a tree which has ever since been call the "fatal trysting tree"   The tree separated just where its immense bole came out of the ground, and formed two large trees

The love affair of these two young people was destined to end in an awful tragedy   Some spy and informer, learning that they had plighted their troth, hastened to inform Alexander Irvine's family of the danger of his misalliance with this beautiful girl, his first love, and he was called back to Edinburgh

The night before he went away he and his sweetheart met, as was usual with them, beneath the trysting tree, and Alexander Irvine gave the girl a knife with a silver handle that had his name engraved, in full, upon it.   They vowed eternal love and parted   In a short time after Irvine returned to Edinburgh he married a Miss Gault, removed to the north of Ireland, where his three sons, Andrew, William and Christopher, were born, and then came to America, some say from Scotland, some from Ireland.   I am not able to say from which country he came, nor does it matter

After he was married a short time, the young Irish girl, to whom he had vowed to be true unto death, heard of his marriage, and one moonlight night she went to the trysting tree and stabbed herself in the heart and died, with the knife of her lover still in the wound   So her brother found her   He drew the knife from her pulseless breast, and holding it aloft, vowed " to never sleep until he plunged the knife, stained by his sister's blood, into Alexander Irvine's heart "

He started that night, in a boat that was to cross the North Channel, but which never landed, and went down with all on board, and rests today beneath the turbid waters that divide Ireland from Scotland

It may be that Alexander Irvine removed from Scotland to the north of Ireland to be further away from the scenes of his early love, and perhaps he crossed the ocean to find ease for his troubled conscience.   Certain it is that tradition has brought to me the story that he was a sad and silent man   He was my ancestor, and his son, Andrew, was my grandfather

Andrew Irvine had many sons, but never named one for his father—
" Alexander being considered an unlucky name " — so I have been told by my
oldest kinswoman now alive   Miss Semple, of Larne, Ireland, in a letter to an
Irvine descendant, says that it was Alexander Irvine first who killed the man on
the hunting field, and not the Alexander who came to Bedford county, Virginia, but she is mistaken, for the story of his misfortune was told by his son,
Andrew, to an old lady, who was born in 1814, and who was alive a year ago

He had three sons — Andrew, Christopher and William   Alexander
Irvine and his wife died the same day   His wife's death grieved him deeply,
but he went with some men into an orchard to have her grave made   He
selected a suitable spot, under a spreading tree, and then returned to his house,
lay down and died without complaining of illness   He and his wife were
buried in one grave   The Virginia Irvines reared Andrew and the Pennsylvania Irvines brought up Christopher and William.   Andrew Irvine was young
when his father died, and, by the time he was grown, he had lost sight of his
two brothers, both younger than himself, and never met them in this life.

Andrew Irvine married Elizabeth Mitchell , Elizabeth Mitchell was the
daughter of William Mitchell and Elizabeth Innes, who were married in Edinburgh, Scotland, and came to Bedford county, Va.   Elizabeth Innes was the
daughter of Hugh Innes, who came to Bedford county, Va , together with his
two brothers — James and Robert.   The ship in which they sailed from Scotland to this country was wrecked, and the Innes brothers — James, Hugh and
Robert were all of the crew that were saved   For many years the descendants
of these three Innes brothers vainly tried to obtain the fortune left by Miss
Jane Innes.

The children of Andrew Irvine and Elizabeth Mitchell, were   Robert,
Stephen, John, Caleb, Joshua, William, Jane, Lucinda, Polly and Elizabeth

It may be stated here that Andrew Irvine was a revolutionary soldier

Robert Irvine died young and unmarried

Stephen married first a Mrs Whitside, widow , second, Betsy Barrier
(maiden name, Janvier) , John married Sarah Wilson , Joshua married a Miss
Wilson , Caleb married Miss Mitchell, and was drowned in the Tennessee
river, Tennessee   He was the grandfather of Wilbur Browder, of Russel-
ville, Ky   William married Eliza Howe , Lucinda married Dr. Flavius Phil-
lips , Jane and Mary married and died young , Elizabeth married Rev Samuel
Rogers, a pioneer preacher of Kentucky

The seven Irvine brothers who came to America before and after the year
1729, were brothers to Margaret Irvine, who married Ephraim McDowell
Their names were : Alexander, George, David, William, Robert, James and
Samuel   As has been stated before, their father and they fled from Scotland
on account of political persecutions   They settled at Gleno, where their
ancestor, Robert Irvine, and his descendants, had owned land since 1584.
The farm i r t   in h t n   d d md mily for   nerations

But they determined to cast aside all superstitious fears and occupy it They made a bleaching green and built a mill in partnership with the McDowells, their kinsmen, and how they prospered shall be told by a lady who recently wrote me a long letter from Larne, Ireland

MOUNTHILL, LARNE, IRELAND

* * * My people have lived here from generation to generation for 300 years * * * The first Irvines came to Gleno, Ireland, in 1584 The McDowells came at the same time They were kinsmen That year a thousand families came from Scotland and the Isles to occupy the land of the Earl of Antrim, and to find safety from persecution There were two brothers of Margaret Irvine McDowell, who fled from the hunting field in Scotland and came in hunting dress in the night-time They found shelter in the house of William Wylie Their names were Alexander and Robert Alexander was pardoned for whatever it was he did and returned to Scotland, and from there he went to America Robert remained and married a daughter of William Wylie, and obtained a grant of land from Lord Antrim Alexander and his brothers and Ephraim McDowell's wife were lineal descendants of Robert Irvine, who fled from Scotland in 1584 Sally, another daughter of William Wylie, married John Knox, a Scottish refugee

The Irvine and McDowell farm has a queer history Altogether you could not look on a more lovely or peaceful spot It went from the first Irvine to whom it belonged, to another and so on, until it was sold to one Francis Lee, in 1731 The way he got the money to buy it was strange He was up rooting some small trees, below one of them he found a pot full of gold coins—with this he bought the farm The Irvines had never had any luck on the farm as long as any member of the family lived on it Lee enlarged the bleaching green and built new works, but he failed in every thing he attempted to do, just as the Irvines had done, and was obliged to sell out A man by the name of Agnew bought the place Then it went to the present owner's grandfather, who killed himself drinking whisky The man who owns it to-day has what we call bad luck His children have nearly all died, and he loses a number of his cattle every year You will think we Irish are superstitious — nevertheless it is quite true, that at certain times around the old mill built by the Irvines and McDowells, a bright light is seen that can not be accounted for It has been seen ever since Alexander Irvine's sweetheart killed herself beneath the trysting tree that overshadowed the mill

There is the largest yew tree ever seen growing before the old home of the Irvines, which was planted by one of the Irvines

From the parish church of Gleno, that stands beside the waterfalls, on the most romantic spot imaginable, overlooking the village, you could speak to one at the old home of the Irvines and McDowells

As I have told you before, the Irvines and McDowells failed in business and went to America — some with Ephraim McDowell and some of them afterwards Seven brothers went, first and last

I have been counting up and I can find 337 souls, dead and alive, that have sprung from Margaret Irvine, wife of Ephraim McDowell, through her son, Thomas McDowell, who married Janet Ried

William Irvine married Anne Craig, in Ireland, issue — Johannah, Christopher and David.

William Irvine buried his only daughter, Johannah, and his wife in the church yard of Raloo, and he and his sons, Christopher and David came to America about 1729, and settled in Bedford county, Virginia

Christopher Irvine, son of William Irvine and Anne Craig, went to Wilkes county, Georgia, and David Irvine married Jane Kyle, July 21, 1754, in Bedford county, Virginia, and came to Kentucky and settled in Madison county He had thirteen children (Sophia, daughter of David Irvine and Jane Kyle, married William Fox Sophia Irvine was a sister to Col William Irvine (who died 1819) and to Capt Christopher, Robert, and Magdalen, who married Pittman. Sophia, who married William Fox, was grandmother of Mrs Sophia Fox Sea, of Louisville, Ky. Sophia was born in 1779 and died in 1833 Amelia married a Hockaday and died in 1830 Mary married Adams and died in 1803 Elizabeth married Hale Talbot. Sally married Goggin Margaret married Mr Pace Jane married Archibald Curle, she was born in 1769 and died 1833 There was also a son, Henry Frances married Rowland Anne married Goggin

Capt Christopher Irvine, born about 1760, was killed while with General Logan in Ohio Captain Christopher married Lydia Calloway, daughter of Col Richard Calloway, who was killed at Boonesboro, Ky. Capt. Christopher Irvine and Lydia Calloway had two daughters, Fannie and Mary, and one son, David Mary (born 1784, died 1869) married John Hart Fannie married Robert Caldwell The widow of Capt. Christopher Irvine married Gen. Richard Hickman

Col William Irvine was born in Campbell county, Virginia, in 1768, died near Richmond, Ky, January 18, 1819. Col William Irvine married Elizabeth Hockaday Issue Christopher, who fell at Dudley's defeat, David, born 1796, Edmund, who married Sally Ann Clay 1823, but died soon after, and his widow married M C Johnston Albert Irvine married Miss Coleman, and, after the death of his wife, removed to Texas Adam married Minerva Stone, and had one son born to him, William McClannahan (born 1825, died 1891), who married his cousin, Elizabeth Irvine. Patsey married Ezekiel Field Amelia married William McClannahan

David, son of Col William Irvine, married Susan McDowell, a granddaughter to Gen Isaac Shelby They had four children (1) Sarah, who married G V   'Who   h i ix children (2) Betts, married

Oliver Patton, (b) Alice, married Dr Gilbert Greenway, (c) Susan, daughter of Sarah, married Judge Richard W Walker, of Alabama Supreme Court. (e) David Irvine, married Lucy Mathews, (f) Newton (2) Isaac Shelby Irvine (3) David W Irvine (4) Elizabeth S Irvine, now of Richmond, Ky, who married William Irvine. The other Irvines to whom the Irvines mentioned are related are Abram Irvine, of Rockbridge county, Virginia, who was born in Ireland (some say Scotland) in 1725, married Mary Dean, born in Ireland in 1734, and had many children John, one of the children (born 1755), came to Kentucky in 1786, and married Miss Armstrong, of Mercer county

The Irvines immigrated to the east of Ireland and west of Scotland with the Gauls of Spain, and our immediate family moved to the North of Ireland during the protectorate of Cromwell On May 9, 1729, some of the Irvines, McDowells, McElroys, Campbells and others sailed from Londonderry and landed the same year in Pennsylvania, where they remained until 1737, when they removed to Rockbridge and Bedford counties, Virginia, and were the first settlers on Burden's grant.

One of the immigrants in that party was John Irvine, a Presbyterian preacher His children were probably all born in this country and consisted of one son, Abram, and four daughters, and probably other sons, but of this I am not certain

---

Irvines and McDowells.

[Copied from Green s " Historic Families of Kentucky "]

Among the very earliest settlers in the valley of Virginia, were Scotch-Irish Presbyterian families, named Irvine, kinsmen of the McDowells and probably descended from the brothers of Ephraim McDowell's wife, who immigrated with him to Pennsylvania and some who followed him to Burden's grant Their names are found among the soldiers of the French and Indian War, as well as the War of the Revolution from both Pennsylvania and Virginia Members of the family were among the first settlers of Mercer county, neighbors to their McDowell kin Among the magistrates who held the first county court in Mercer, in August, 1786, were John Irvine, Samuel McDowell Sr , and Gabriel Madison One of the family, Anna, daughter of Abram Irvine, became the wife of her kinsman, Samuel McDowell, of Mercer The children born of this marriage were John Adair, soldier in the War of 1812, married Lucy Todd Starling, daughter of William Starling and Susannah Lyne, of Mercer county, Ky His daughter, Anne, married John Winston Price, of Hillsboro, Ohio

Abram _____ born April 24, 1792, soldier in the War of 1812 fought at

Missisenewa, was clerk of the Supreme Court, of the Court of Common Pleas, and of the Court in Banc and was at one time mayor of Columbus, Ohio   He married Eliza Seldon, in 1817, daughter of Colonel Lord. Gen Irvine McDowell, of the United States army, who attained the highest rank of any of his name, was his oldest son. Col. John McDowell. soldier in the Union army, was another son. Malcolm McDowell, also a soldier in the Union army, was another son, while his daughter, Eliza, married Major Bridgeman, of the regular army

Col Joseph McDowell married Sarah Irvine, sister to Anna Irvine, wife of Samuel McDowell   Samuel, son of Col Joseph Irvine and Sarah Irvine McDowell, married first, Amanda Ball, granddaughter of John Reed, and cousin to James G Birney   The sole issue of this marriage was a daughter, who married Dr Meyer, of Boyle county, Ky.

Information Concerning the Irvines from San Antonio, Texas.

Abram Irvine, born in Scotland, May 1725, married Mary Dean, born in Ireland, February 22, 1733. They emigrated to Rockbridge county, Virginia Mary Dean's mother was Jane McAlister, a Scotch woman who assisted at the siege of Londonderry   The Protestants were reduced to starvation, and Jane McAlister inverted the flour barrels and made the tops white with flour in order that the spies might think that article plentiful when they looked through the cracks of the weak walls

The children of Abram Irvine and Mary Dean were John, born February 25, 1755, married Prudence Armstrong, of Mercer county, Kentucky   The children of John and Prudence Armstrong Irvine were Samuel, Polly, Margaret, Sally, Abram, Priscilla and Robert

Hans, born April 25, 1758, never married

Margaret Irvine, born April 25, 1762, married, first, Samuel Lapsley, second, Rev John Lyle

Mary Irvine married, first, William Adair, second, Issachar Paulding. Her children were Alexander and William Adair

Anne Irvine, born November 28, 1763, married Samuel McDowell. Their children were John, Abram, William, Joseph, Sally, Reed and Alexander

Abram Irvine, born August 8, 1766, married, first, Sally Henry, and second, Margaret McAfee

Robert Irvine, born in 1768, married Judith Glover   Children : John, Polly, Judith. Abram D , Robert and Sarah

Nancy Irvine, born July 5, 1790, married Frank McMordie   Children Robert, Jane, Hans, Polly, Abram and Margaret

Eliza, born in 1766, married George Caldwell, grandfather of Mrs Mary Caldwell Crawford, of San Antonio, Texas. The children of Elizabeth Irvine and George Caldwell were George, Polly, Abram, Isabella, John, William and Eliza

Sarah Irvine, born November 21, 1774, married Joseph McDowell Children Sarah, Margaret, Lucy, Charles, Caleb and Magdalen, who is last living one of this generation, and is now Mrs M M Wallace, and lives near Danville, Ky

William Dean Irvine, born August, 1775, never married Was captain of volunteers in the War of 1812, died in Natchez, Miss.

William Irvine and Some of His Descendants.

William Irvine married Anne Craig in Ireland Issue Johannah, who died and lies buried in the old churchyard of Raloo, Ireland, Christopher and David

Miss Semple, who lives at Mounthill, Larne, Ireland, writes

"I have found the old book of a stone-cutter, which is two hundred years old He was in the habit of going to persons, who were entitled to coats of arms, and asking the privilege of copying their arms, in order to carve them on the tombstones of the dead I send you the arms of William Irvine, given to this old stone cutter "

Miss Semple then sends the arms of one branch of the Irvines of Bonshaw—motto "Sub sole sub umbra virens " These arms may have been chosen by William Irvine, but they are not the arms belonging to the Irish branch Sir William d'Arcey Irvine was kind enough to send me the arms borne by the branch of the family of the house of Bonshaw, that settled in Ireland, and they appear in the front of this book

William Irvine's wife, Anne Craig, died and was buried at Raloo, and he and his two sons, David and Christopher, came to America, landed at Philadelphia, and from thence made their way to Bedford county, Virginia, and settled. Christopher Irvine, son of William Irvine and Anne Craig, removed from Bedford county, Virginia, to Wilkes county, Georgia, and David came to Kentucky, and was the progenitor of the Madison county Irvines

The will of David Irvine, son of William and Anne Craig, was written in 1804 and recorded in 1805 Heirs Mary, Elizabeth, Magdalen, Anna, William, Sarah, Jane, Robert, Frances, Margaret, Amelia, Sophia, Christopher, (who died before the will was made) Sophia married William Fox, Amelia married Hockaday, Mary married Adams, Elizabeth married Hale Talbot, Sarah married Goggin, Margaret married Pace, Jane married Archibald Curle, Frances married Rowland, Anne married Goggin, and Captain Christopher was killed when about Concord Church in Ohio

William, son of David Irvine, married Elizabeth Hockaday William came from Campbell county, Virginia, died in Richmond, Ky, in 1819, aged fifty-five years His wife died in 1818. William Irvine was the first clerk of the court of Madison county, Kentucky He was appointed clerk by the first court that was organized in that county, and held the office until his death

His brother, Christopher, built the fort at Irvine's Lick. He was badly wounded at Little Mountain Christopher was a delegate to the convention in Virginia in 1787–88, that ratified the Constitution of the United States, also delegate to the Danville, Ky, convention, elector of the United States Senate in 1792, district presidential elector in 1805 and 1817, elector at large in 1813, member of the Kentucky Society for Promoting Useful Knowledge Christopher Irvine had eleven children I am able to give the names of only seven — David, Christopher, Albert, Edwin, Adam, Mrs Ezekiel Field and Mrs Wm McClannahan.

David, son of William Irvine, married a daughter of Dr. Ephraim McDowell and his wife — Shelby, daughter of first governor of Kentucky, Isaac Shelby. (The wife of Governor Shelby was a daughter of Nathaniel Hart, who was a distinguished member of the Transylvania Company and brother of Mrs Henry Clay's father, and of United States Senator Archibald Dickson's grandfather)

David Irvine was born 1796, died 1872 Children David, Irvine Shelby, Sarah and Elizabeth The last, Elizabeth, married her cousin, W M Irvine, son of Adam Irvine Sarah married Hon Addison White Christopher was a captain in the War of 1812, he was killed at Fort Meigs and there buried Edwin, or Edmund, married Sarah Ann, daughter of Gen Green Clay, sister of Gen Cassius M Clay, after the death of Edwin Irvine she married Mat. Johnson, distinguished financier of Lexington, Ky

Albert, son of David Irvine, was a minister, his son, Adam, is a ranchman at Gainesville, Tex

Christopher Irvine, brother of William, builder of Fort Irvine and first clerk of Madison county, Ky, was a delegate to the Danville convention, in 1785, and deputy surveyor of Lincoln county, Ky, before the formation of Madison, together with Gen Green Clay He was also a member of the Lincoln county court in 1783, he was killed during an Indian raid in Ohio, in 1786 The wife of this Christopher was Lydia, daughter of Col Richard Calloway, Lydia's second husband was Gen Richard Hickman The daughter of Gen Richard Hickman and Lydia Calloway, married Samuel Hanson, and their son Roger Hanson, was the famous commander of the Orphan Brigade in the Confederate army Richard Hanson, lawyer of Paris, Ky, was a son of Samuel Hanson, and the daughter of Gen. R. Hickman and Lydia Calloway, his wife, a daughter of Samuel Hanson married Captain Stern, soldier in the Mexican War

Col Christopher Irvine and his wife Lydia Calloway had three children:

David C ; Fanny, who married Robert Caldwell, Mary, who married John Hart, of Fayette county, Ky David C, married a Miss Howard, of Fayette county, Ky To her is due the honor of founding the first temperance society in Madison county, Ky She was a very talented woman

Christopher Irvine, brother of David, son of William the widower, married, late in life, Jane, widow of Col John Hardin, who was killed by Indians while on a peace mission under the government, beyond the Ohio river

The children of Francis Irvine Caldwell, daughter of Col Christopher Irvine and his wife, Lydia Calloway, were· James, a minister, David C, who moved to Missouri, Mary, who married Chief Justice Simpson, of Winchester, Ky, and Elizabeth, who married Orville Browning, of Illinois

Mrs. Edmund Pendleton Shelby, of Lexington, Ky, is descended from Mary Irvine (daughter of Col Christopher Irvine and his wife, Lydia Calloway), who married John Hart The children of Mary Irvine and John Hart, were David, who married Lucy Ann Goodloe, the children of this marriage were Edwin, Christopher, Sophia, Isaac, Fanny, John, David, Lydia, Mary Thomas, Sallie and Nathaniel The children of David Hart, who married Lucy Ann Goodloe, are Susan Goodloe, who married Edmund Pendleton Shelby Their children are Hart William, Lucy, Lily F. Edmund, David, Isaac, Evan, Susan, Mary and Arthur Lily Fontaine Shelby married George Sea Shanklin, issue—Shelby and George

Genealogy of Mrs Sophia Fox Sea, of Louisville, Ky —Mrs Sea is well known in literary circles as a writer of great ability She proves the saying that has been in the Irvine family for generations — " The Irvine women have ever been more brilliant and talented than the men "

DAVID IRVINE was born May 29, 1721, he died October 17, 1804 On July 21, 1754, in Bedford county, Virginia, he was married by the Rev McKee, to Jane Kyle, who died February 15, 1809 Thirteen children

1. Christopher, born September 11, 1755, killed by Indians in Ohio, about October 6, 1786. He married Lydia Calloway, daughter of Colonel Richard Calloway He left three children, Mary, Fannie and David C Mary was born in Madison county, Kentucky, March 4, 1784, married John Hart, and died in Fayette county, Kentucky, September 14, 1869. Fannie married Robert Caldwell

2. Mary, born September 15, 1757, married Christopher (?) Adams, died February 22, 1803

3. Elizabeth, born January 5, 1760, married Hale Talbot, and died

4. Anne, born May 18, 1761, married Richard Goggin September 28, 1791, and died

5. William, born in Campbell county, Virginia, June 2, 1763; married Elizabeth Hockaday, died in Madison county, Kentucky, January
   •   18,

6   Magdalene, born July 6, 1765, married (1) Bourne Price, December 26, 1787, (2) —— Pittman, died January 25, 1830

7   Sarah, born January 9, 1767, married —— Goggin, and died about 1832

8   Jane, born July 2, 1769, married Archibald Curle, September 29, 1791, died July —, 1833

9   Robert, born March —, 1771, died October —, 1818

10 Frances, born —— 21st, 177-, married —— Rowland, and died

11 Margaret, born April 6, 1774, married John Page December 18, 179—, died August 2, 1860

12 Amelia born June 25, 1775; married Isaac Hockaday, March 31, 1796, died July 13, 1830

13 Sophie born December 11, 1779, married William Fox,* May 13, 1802, died in Somerset, Ky, October 15, 1833

The foregoing is taken from David Irvine's family Bible, the record is now with Mrs Sophie Boyd. This is a correct copy

A M SFA, JR, 1895

The Fox Line.

The Fox family that settled in Virginia is of the same lineage as Henry, Lord Holland, and retain to this day many strongly marked racial characteristics   Of the latter family sprung WILLIAM FOX, son of Samuel Fox and Rhoda Pickering Fox. William Fox was born in Hanover county, Va, March 1, 1779 He apprenticed himself to his uncle, Peter Tinsley, clerk of the High Court of Chancery, and it was to Mr Tinsley that he was indebted for his fine penmanship and knowledge of jurisprudence   From 1799 until his resignation in 1846, he was clerk of the Pulaski County and Circuit Courts His opinions, bearing upon knotty points of law, were accepted as incontrovertible authority by all the leading lawyers of his district   He was a man of inherited aristocratic social theories, but of exalted personal worth, of the highest order of intellectual and business finesse second to none   He married Sophie Irvine, youngest daughter of David Irvine and Jane Kyle, a worthy descendant of her ancient line of intellectual and virtuous gentlewomen. Sophie Irvine died October 15, 1833 William Fox married, second, Mary Irvine, daughter of Hale and Elizabeth (Irvine) Talbot, of Warren county, Mo The children of William Fox and Sophie Irvine were:

I FONTAINE TALBOT   (See I below)

Willia T   · · ····· ·· ··· H· f·ther w·· I·d·· T·· ·· ·· F Fox, of Danville, K

II AMANDA FITZALAN, who married her cousin, Bourne Goggin, also
a descendent of the Irvines   Campbell speaks of the Goggin family thus
The family of Gookin, or Goggin, is very ancient, and appears to have
been originally found at Canterbury in Kent, England   The name has
undergone successive changes — the early New England (Virginia) chroni-
cles spelled it "Goggin"   Daniel Goggin came to Virginia 1621, with
fifty picked men of his own, and thirty passengers exceedingly well fur-
nished with all sorts of provisions, cattle, etc , and planted himself at
Newport News   In the massacre of 1622 he held out against the savages,
with a force of thirty men, and saved his plantation   It is possible that
he affected to make a settlement independent of the civil power of the
colony, and it appears to have been styled by his son, "a lordship
It was above Newport News, and called Mary s Mount   Their ancient
crest is given by Campbell   Bourne Goggin and Amanda F Goggin
had four children ·
    1 William, banker, married to Katherine Higgins   They have
       children
    2 Ann, married to Timothy Pennington   They have five children
       Bessie, Bourne, Ephraim, Amanda Fox, who married Philip
       Kemp (railroad official), and Timothy
    3 Richard, deceased, also married Katherine Higgins, and left two
       children   Bourne and Jeannie
    4 Amanda Fitzalan, unmarried
III. JANE PICKERING, who married, first Dr James Caldwell, and second,
Eben Milton, Esq   By Dr Caldwell she had four children
    1 Sophie Irvine, married to Dr James Parker   They had four
       children   Samuel, Joseph, Zenice and Tea
    2 Mary, who married Sy Richardson   No children
    3. Isabella, unmarried
    4 Amanda Fitzalan, deceased
IV ELIZABETH FOX, married to —— Fitzpatrick, and had three children
    1 Sophie, married to Thompson Miller, of Missouri
    2. Mary.
    3 James
 V. SOPHIE IRVINE, married to Col John S. Kendrick, a Virginia gen-
tleman   She left one child
    Sophie, married to Judge Jas. W Alcorn, of Stanford, Ky , a cor-
      poration lawyer of high standing   They have a number of
      children
VI WILLIAM MONTGOMERY, married Sophionia Coffee   They had
seven children
    1 Jesse, married Jane Newell, and has five children.
    2 I ·

3 William, unmarried.

4 Bourne, married Nannie Wood, and has two children

5 Frank, deceased

6 Montgomery, married Anne Baughman, and has two children

1 FONTAINE TALBOT FOX (No. 1 above), late Judge of the Eighth
Kentucky circuit, of Danville, Ky Judge Fox spent a long life in public
service, having filled many important offices of public trust, and in every
capacity manifesting that incorruptible integrity, the inherited ruling principle of his nature He made a large fortune at the legitimate practice of
the law, having been retained as leading counsel in nearly all the most
famous suits filed in the courts of Kentucky in his day, his fine oratorical
powers and keen wit rendering him invulnerable in argument At his his
toric home near Danville, Ky , he entertained with almost princely lavish-
ness His name is a synonym throughout his native state for legal learning
and acumen and exalted personal worth He married Eliza Hunton,
daughter of Thomas and Ann (Bell) Hunton, of Charlottesville, Va. Mrs
Fox springs from renowned English and American ancestry Among the
possessions of the Hunton family is a coat of arms granted the family by
Queen Elizabeth, in consideration of a large money loan. She is a cousin
of General Eppa Hunton, U S Senator from Virginia, and of electoral
commission fame Her three brothers, Felix, Logan and Thomas Hunton,
form a coterie of legal lights rarely ever found in one family, Logan
Hunton having been the author of the Allison letter to which is accredited
the election of Taylor to the presidency In consideration of this fact he
was offered a cabinet position, but declined the honor, unwilling to give
up his large and lucrative practice at the New Orleans bar, but accepted
the position of attorney for the District of Louisiana Thomas Hunton
was his law partner In Missouri, during the stormy days preceding the
civil war, Felix Hunton, although a cripple from rheumatism, by virtue of
his splendid intellect and executive finesse, was the leader of the Democratic party, and could easily have had any office within the gift of the
people Mrs. Fox's maternal grandfather was John Bell, a Virginian, and
a man of large wealth, who came to Kentucky at an early day He
married Frances Tunstall, a lineal descendant of the famous English family
by that name There is in the possession of the Tunstall family a paper
prepared by Froude, the English historian, whose mother was a Tunstall,
tracing the Tunstall line through hundreds of years down to the immigration
to this country, a valuable document supplemented by the American branch
The children of Fontaine Talbot Fox and Eliza Hunton Fox are

1. Thomas Hunton, lawyer and brilliant writer He married Henrietta
Clay Wilson, a widow, née Gist, a descendant of the Gist family
so famous in colonial and pioneer history She died in 1889
II married of Mary McNeely of ed the Kentucky

family By his first wife he had two children, Susan Gist, unmarried, and Eliza Hunton, who married John Rogers, a farmer of Fayette county, Kentucky and has two children, William and Thomas Hunton Rogers

2 William McKee Fox, deceased, a lawyer of distinguished ability and magnetic personality, invariably retained as counsel in every suit filed in his large and important judicial district   Unmarried

3 Peter Camden Fox, deceased, lawyer, and Major of Scott's Louisiana Cavalry, on the Southern side, during the war between the states, a man of strong mental endowments, and also of great magnetic personality   Unmarried

4 Fontaine Talbot Fox, lawyer, of Louisville, Ky., was assistant city attorney of Louisville, from 1870 to 1873   Appointed by Governor McCreary vice-chancellor   Ran for governor of Kentucky on the Prohibition ticket in 1887   Is author of two books, on the "The Warranty in the Fire Insurance Contract," and the "Woman Suffrage Movement in the United States"   Is called a master of the English language   He married Mary Barton, daughter of Prof Samuel Barton and Frances Pierce DuRelle, a widow, mother of Judge DuRelle, of the Supreme Court of Kentucky   Professor Barton was closely allied to the Key family of Maryland, and his wife is a member of the Pierce family of which President Pierce was the head   Judge and Mrs Fox had five children   Fontaine, Frances, S Barton, Mary Yandell and Jessie St John

5 Samuel Irvine Fox, a physician, residing in Montgomery county, Texas, who married Margaret Derrick, of a fine old South Carolina family   They have four children   Carrie Eliza, Margaret, Fontaine Talbot and Annie

6 Felix Goggin Fox, lawyer, and a man of scholarly attainments

7 Sophie Irvine Fox, married to Capt Andrew McBrayer Sea. Mrs Sea is a writer who has left her impress in poetry and prose on the literature of her time   Captain Sea is a descendant of pioneer families, and of the ancient Scotch-Irish race of McBriar or McBrayer. (See Anderson's "Scottish Nation.") He is a commission merchant of Louisville, and an elder in the Presbyterian Church, the Church of his covenanting ancestry   Was a Confederate soldier, and won his spurs on hotly-contested fields   Captain and Mrs Sea have four sons. Fontaine Fox, Robert Winston, Andrew McBrayer and Logan Hunton. Captain Sea's father, Robert W Sea, was a wealthy merchant of Lawrenceburg, Ky., a man who stood very high in the community   It is said of him that he nearly put an end to litigation in his county people going

3

to him to settle their differences rather than to the courts   He
married Mary McBrayer, daughter of Andrew McBrayer and
Martha (Blackwell) McBrayer, and died at the early age of thirty-
five, in 1845   In the Biographical Encyclopedia of Kentucky, is
a statement to the effect that Wm McBrayer, father of Andrew
McBrayer, came, in 1775, to Kentucky from North Carolina,
to which state he had immigrated from Ireland just prior to the
Revolutionary War   Leonard Sea, paternal grandfather of Captain Sea, was a soldier in General Wayne's army and distinguished
for bravery in the battle of Fort Meigs and other bloody engage-
ments

8. John Oliver Fox, a civil engineer, was employed in important
work in several large European and American cities. He died
in 1876, aged twenty-nine years

9. Ann Bell Fox, married to Jerry Clemens Caldwell, a successful
stock-raiser and able financier, a man of large wealth   He is a
descendant of the Wickliffe, Caldwell and Clemens families of
Kentucky   They have five children   Charles Wickliffe, Eliza
Hunton, Jerry Clemens, Fontaine Fox and Logan

10. Charles Crittenden Fox, lawyer, is city attorney at Danville, Ky ,
and master commissioner of the Boyle Circuit Court, and an elder
in the Presbyterian Church   His standing at the bar of Kentucky
is second to none   He married Mary Allen, daughter of Albert
Allen and Mary (Offutt) Allen, of Lexington, and niece of
Madison C Johnston, the celebrated jurist, nephew of Col
Richard M Johnson, vice-president of the United States. They
have three living children   Allen, Anne Bell and Mary Hunton
Samuel Fox, father of William Fox, married Rhoda Pickering,
daughter of Richard and Lucy Pickering, at Richmond, Va ,
date unknown   He came to Kentucky about 1783   It is said
he inherited a large tract of land under the Virginia law of
primogeniture   He owned a large estate and many slaves in
Madison county, Ky , where Foxtown is now located,   He died
at Fox's, the name of his place, July 9, 1844, aged nearly ninety-
nine years

THE SCOTCH-IRISH RACE.

SOPHIE IRVINE FOX SEA

Fair, those historic hills and valleys, where
  The shamrock and thistle grew,
Where over the slopes and battle crowned heights
  The breath of the heather blew

And a green isle shone clear as a jewel
    In setting of crystal dew,
But fairer the light of immortal deeds
    That shine eternal through

Illumined in the dim fane of ages,
    God's thinkers and workers stand
He calleth them, as the chieftain calleth
    Trusty ones in his command,
To lead in the brunt of the combat
    With foes on every hand
As such we cry, Hail, comrades, and welcome,
    Welcome to our dear Southland!

Yes, all hail to the race whose childhood saw
    God's truth like a rushlight shine,
Till Iona's grim walls, on Scotia's shore,
    Glowed with effulgence divine
Still that light shines like the stars' fixed splendor,
    Still the great heart of mankind
Reaches to it, through the mist of ages,
    Claims its heritage sublime

True hearts, of old Irish fire was your flame
    Akindled at Tara's shrine,
And nourished by Scottish strength of will,
    Rare union of soul and mind,
Something akin to the power that holds
    In check the wave and the wind
Was that dauntless race that no fear could tame,
    No earthly fetters could bind

And worthy they of all hearts' true homage,
    Worthy they that which is best
And grandest and noblest in words that burn
    In thoughts to this sad earth blest
Statesmen, soldiers, God's thinkers, God's workers,
    To-day they stand well-confessed,
As men in manhood's broadest manliness,
    Women by womanhood's test

O, land, our land, withhold not thy fulness
    Of honor   To death they wore,
Like a garment well-fitting, thy purpose,
    For thy weal their blood did pour
Withhold not thy love   These spirits of fire
    Upward like angels did soar,
Those wills of iron akindled the flame
    Of liberty on this shore

Still the fire burneth, we thank Thee, O God!
    Truth, virtue, their guiding star
Tenderest when humanity calls them,
    Sublime st in their l f

Hail, hail, green isle, in thy crystal setting,
Hail, stern rock-bound coast afar,
Our birthrights of historic memories
Glorious, eternal are

(Copied from "Cabells and Their Kin," history written by the eminent
historian and writer of Nelson county, Virginia — Mr Alexander Brown)

Irvines.

Clementia Cabell, born February 26, 1794, married at Union Hill, June
29, 1815, Jesse Irvine, of Bedford county, Va , died at Otter, residence of her
husband, near Peaks of Otter, June 12, 1841   Her husband, Jesse Irvine, was
born in Bedford county, Va , 1792, educated at Washington Academy, 1810,
and died February 2 1876   He was the son of Wm and Martha Burton
Irvine   The father, Wm Irvine, died in Bedford county, Va , in 1829   He
was among the early settlers of that county   There were three brothers, David,
Christopher and William Irvine, who are said to have come originally from
Ireland, i e , to have been Scotch-Irish   Date of David's death unknown.
Christopher died in 1769, and William in 1767   The widow of William Irvine
married Robert Coman, of the same family as Wm Coman, opposing lawyer
to Patrick Henry in the beef case of Hook vs. Venable   Christopher's son,
William, who is mentioned in his will, but William (died in 1829) is said to
have been the son of first William, who died in 1767   Capt Christopher and
Col William Irvine, who removed to Kentucky about 1779, were sons of one
of the three emigrant brothers   Mrs Clementia Cabell Irvine had issue by
Jesse Irvine, her husband, as follows. Wm Cabell (died in infancy), Martha
(died in infancy), Ann C , Elvira Bruce (died young), Edward C , Sarah Cabell,
Patrick Cabell, born in 1827, became a physician died October 18, 1854, unmarried   Margaret, born 1829, died 1830, Mary Eliza, Jesse, Juliet M ,
Margaret Frances   Wm Cabell Irvine, lawyer, married Mary Ann Lewis,
daughter of Meriwether Lewis, of Milton, N C , died childless after being married three years   Wm Cabell Irvine removed to California, where he died in
1851   Meriwether Lewis, of Milton, N. C , was a son of Robert Lewis and his
wife, Ann Ragland   Robert Lewis was a son of Major James Lewis and his wife,
Mildred Lewis   Major James Lewis was born October 8, 1720   Major James
Lewis was the son of Col Charles Lewis, born 1696, married in 1717, Mary
Howell, settled "The Bird" plantation in Goochland county, April 17, 1733–
1779. Anne C , a descendant of these, is still living   She married, first,
March 26, 1845, David Flournoy son of Dr David Flournoy, of Prince Edward
county, Va a widower with six children   Dr David Flournoy died Novem-
ber 11, · ·   having, one child by his wife Anne C Irvine Sarah Irvine

Flournoy, born 1846, died 1849 Mrs. Anne C Irvine Flournoy married, second, March 12, 1848, J Overby, Esq , a farmer of Prince Edward county, Va , a descendant of an old English family Left seven children at his death.

Paul Carrington Cabell, born April 10, 1799, educated at " Union Hill " until 1813, lived with Dr Geo Calloway in Lynchburg, Va , and went to school to Holcombe and Jones in 1813–14 and to John Reid in 1814–15 Studied medicine under Dr Calloway, a distinguished physician of Amherst county Married June 12, 1823, Mary B Irvine, daughter of Wm Irvine, of Bedford county, Va , vestryman of Lexington parish, died June 9, 1836, buried at " Mountain View " His wife died at Lynchburg, July, 1857, and was buried by her husband The children of Paul Carrington Cabell and his wife, Mary B Irvine, were Wm Irvine, Anne Carrington, Martha Elizabeth (who died young), Sallie Massie, Martha Burton (born 1833, died 1834), and Paul Clement.

Higginbotham.

Margaret Washington Cabell, married first, December 7, 1815, at "Soldier's Joy," John Higginbotham, who died February 23, 1822 Issue William, Thomas and Laura, born 1819, died 1827 Mrs Margaret W. Higginbotham, married second, September 17, 1839, at Lynchburg, Va , Dr Nathaniel West Payne, of Amherst county, Va , whose oldest daughter by his first marriage, was the wife of Wm A S Cabell, son of S Cabell Mrs Payne died February 17, 1887, without issue by her second husband, who was the son of Col Philip Payne and his wife, Eliza Dandridge, a descendant of Gov John West, one of the founders of Virginia Col Philip Payne was a son of Col John Payne, of Whitehall, frequently member of the house of Burgesses from Goochland, who died 1774 Col John Payne was a son of George Payne, sheriff of Goochland, who died in 1874, and his wife, Mary Woodson, daughter of Robert Woodson and his wife, Elizabeth Ferris, of " Curls "

On October 6, 1783, Wm Cabell, Jr , was appointed surveyor of Amherst county, by William and Mary College, filled this office until December 1, 1788

Tuckers.

Sarah Cabell Irvine, born October 17, 1825, married November 25, 1846, by Rev Jacob Mitchell, to Asa D Dickinson, of Prince Edward county, Va Asa D Dickinson was born at " Inverness," Nottoway county, Va , March 31, 1816, prepared for coll J D l Comf   ad ated from Hampden-

Sidney College, September, 1836, attended lectures at William and Mary College, under Judge Beverly Tucker, in law , and under President Thos R Dew, in political economy in 1837-38, located at Prince Edward Courthouse in 1838, to practice his profession and soon attained a position of full practice at law.

Cornelia Rives, married first, in 1866, to Charles Harrison, son of Prof Gessner Harrison, of the University of Virginia, by his wife, Eliza Tucker, daughter of Prof George Tucker and his wife. Maria Ball Carter. Charles Harrison and his wife Cornelia Rives, had no issue After the death of Charles Harrison, his widow, Cornelia Rives, married Mr Wilborne, and has one child — Elizabeth Rives

The first wife of George Rives was Mary Eliza, daughter of Robert Carter, of " Redlands," and his wife, Mary Coles, sister of Edward Coles, the first governor of Illinois. and a daughter of John Coles (1745–1808), and his wife, Rebecca E Tucker (1750–1826). Robert Carter, son of Edward Carter and Sarah Champe, his wife Edward C was the son of second John Carter and Elizabeth Hill John Carter was the son of Robert Carter, alias King Carter, of Crotomon The children of Mary Eliza Carter and George Rives were : Robert, who died unmarried, George Cabell and James Henry. George Rives married, second, at University of Virginia, March 31, 1806, Maria Farley Tucker, who survived him many years Maria Farley Tucker was the daughter of Prof George Tucker, born 1775, in the Bermudas, came to Virginia and was a member of the Virginia Legislature and of the United States House of Representatives from Virginia, 1818–25, professor in University of Virginia, 1825-45, and author of numerous books , died April 10, 1861 The wife of Prof. George Tucker was Maria Ball Carter, and was a daughter of the only daughter of General George Washington's only sister Thus, Maria Farley Rives was a great grandniece to George Washington, and inherited many precious memorials. She bore her husband four children, viz George Tucker, born ——, married 1843, at University of Virginia , in 1860 lieutenant in C S A ; taken prisoner at Roanoake Island , exchanged , unanimously elected captain of a company , fell while gallantly leading a charge made by Wise's brigade near Petersburg, March 29, 1865 , never was married Eleanor Rives, living, has Edward Rives, University of Virginia, 1863-67. B L , a lawyer, died May 22, 1877, in his twenty-seventh year , unmarried Lawrence Alexander Rives, University of Virginia, 1868 69, died at Little Rock, Ark , January 5, 1873, in his twenty-second year

Mary Rives married William Eaton, vestryman of old Blandford church, near Petersburg, removed, with other members of his family, to North Carolina, in 1725 where he became a very prominent man Their son, Thomas Eaton, married Anna Bland, sister to Frances Bland, who married, first, John Randolph and became the mother of John Randolph, of Roanoake After the death of Hon Thomas Eaton his widow married Judge St George Tucker, issue, Judge Henry St George, and Nathaniel Beverly. See ' The Life Influence and

Services of James Jones White," by Hon John Randolph Tucker (only mention made)

From the diary of the late Major Cabell, of "Union Hill," February 7, 1856 "The interment of Joseph C Cabell took place to-day at 12 o'clock, buried in his garden at Edgwood, by the side of Judge St George Tucker and his wife, and Miss Parke Carter"

Mrs Mary W Cabell, widow of the late Joseph C Cabell (no children) was the daughter of George Carter, Esq, of Lancaster, and his wife, Lelia, daughter of Sir Peyton Skipwith, Baronet After the death of her first husband, Mrs Lelia Skipwith married Judge St George Tucker, October 8, 1791 Mr Tucker was a widower, having lost his wife, Mrs Frances Bland Randolph, mother of John Randolph, of Roanoake

---

Hon. J. Proctor Knott.

This distinguished gentleman, whose name graces the head of this sketch, is descended from the Irvines as follows Abram Irvine, a descendant of the house of Bonshaw and resident of the north of Ireland, came to this country some time before the War of the Revolution—the exact date his descendants have been unable to learn He settled in Virginia and there married Mary Dean. He removed from Virginia to Kentucky some time between the years 1780 and 1790, and made his home in Boyle county, near Danville, Ky., within a few miles of Governor Shelby's residence Abram Irvine and his wife, Mary Dean, had nine children

Abram Irvine was the son of Rev John Irvine Mary Irvine, daughter of Abram Irvine and Mary Dean, his wife, married Samuel M Elroy. Their son, William E M'Elroy, married Keturah Cleland Their daughter, Maria Irvine M'Elroy, married Joseph Percy Knott. Issue

1 William T, who married Marian Briggs M Elroy, and after her death married Mrs Lydia M'Elroy (née Harrison), widow of Rev Hugh Sneed M'Elroy

2 Keturah Frances, married to Wells Rawlings (long since deceased)

3 Samuel Cleland, married Miss Sarah Gates, of Georgia

4 Marian Margaret, married to Robert T Nesbit

5 Edward Whitfield, married Miss Mattie C M'Koy (M'Coy)

6 Anne Maria, married to John Randolph Hudnell

7 Joanne, married to Rev Marcellus G Gavin, of St. Louis, Mo.

8 James Proctor, married Sarah Rosanna M'Elroy.

James Proctor Knott was born August 27, 1830, married June 14, 1858 Elected to the Mis or [illegible] attorney-general of the same state August, 1859, and elected to that office August, 1860   Returned to Kentucky in 1862, elected to the fortieth Congress in 1867, forty-first, 1868; forty-fourth, 1874, and re elected successively to the forty-fifth, forty sixth and forty-seventh   Elected Governor of Kentucky August, 1883, and to the constitutional convention in August, 1890

Governor Knott, writes   "I know very little of my father's ancestry of that name   The records were destroyed in the burning of my grandmother's residence, when I was a small boy   All I know is that my grandfather, my great-grandfather and my great-great-grandfather were all only sons, and all of them, except my grandfather, were ministers of the Church of England , that they were of Danish extraction, and lived in Northumberland, England,— I mean their forebears, down to the immigration of my grandfather's grandfather, who was a curate on that estate (in Northumberland) , and that I know by tradition only   There is a tradition, also, that the last-named, married a daughter of Earl Percy and in that way the name Percy, which was borne by my father, my grandfather and my great grandfather came into the family, but I never thought it worth while to ascertain

"I was once assured by a painstaking antiquary that he had traced my father's side of the house to Richard de Percy in a direct line, one of the grim old barons appointed at Runnymede to see that John Lackland should observe the Great Charta of English liberty there extorted from him, and that my coat of arms is Or a lion rampant, az   I am a Scotch-Irishman, however, and with many of the traits of that race, I have inherited the sentiment 'that blood is thicker than water,' and, whether pleb or patrician, I am always glad to recognize my kinsfolk."

In appearance, Governor Knott is of a very uncommon type of manhood He is a little above medium height, is strongly and compactly built   At the first glance one is impressed by strength—mental and physical   He is not one with whom a stranger would attempt to converse uninvited, and yet those who know him well say that he is the kindest and most gentle of men to women and children, and is charitable almost to a fault   As proof of his mental capacity I subjoin his speech—known all over the world as "The Duluth Speech "   It has been published again and again in this country, and has been translated into many languages   The school boys, by thousands, have recited it and murdered its inimitable humor and fadeless and matchless fancies ever since it first came before the public in 1871   It is needless to say, to one who reads it, that it will glow in the praises of men forever

Col. R. T. Irvine,

Residing at Big Stone Gap, Virginia, writes

I have a very interesting letter from Dr. Hervy McDowell, of Cynthiana, Ky., dated May 7, 1893, in which, among other things, he says "that the name Irvine is a very old surname in Scotland and was originally Erevine and derived from the Celtic erin-vine or fein, eiin meaning west, and vine or fein a strong or resolute man, and they immigrated to the east of Ireland, and west of Scotland with the Gauls of Spain, and that our immediate family moved to the north of Ireland during the reign of Cromwell "—History of Scotland On May 9, 1729, some of the Irvines, McDowells, McElroys, Campbells and others sailed from Londonderry and landed the same year in Pennsylvania, where they remained until 1737, when they moved to Rockbridge county, Virginia, and were the first settlers on Burden's grant

One of the immigrants in that party was John (or James?) Irvine, a Presbyterian preacher   Dr. McDowell says that his children were probably all born in this country and consisted of one son, Abram, and four daughters, and probably other sons, but of this he is not certain   This is all the information bearing directly on the Irvines that I get from Dr McDowell's letter   The remainder of it is devoted chiefly to the various marriages between the Irvines and McDowells.

I will now take up as you suggest and give the names of the descendants of Abram Irvine, the son of Rev John (or James?) Irvine, the immigrant.   But first, I would state that of the four sisters of this Abram Irvine, three married McElroys, and from them sprang the numerous families of that name in Marion and Washington counties and in that part of the state, including the mother of ex-Governor Knott   The fourth sister never married   Abram Irvine was born in Scotland, May, 1725   He married Mary Dean, who was born in Ireland, February 22, 1733   Both had immigrated with their parents to Rockbridge county, Va

(Note —Another account I have says that Abram Irvine was born in Rockbridge county, Va, in 1731, and died June 1, 1814, and that Mary Dean was born in Rockbridge county, Va, January 1, 1733, and died in 1801   I think the account I have adopted above is correct as to the times and places of their births.   Certainly neither of them was born in Virginia, as the McDowells and Irvines did not go from western Pennsylvania to " Burden's grant" in Rockbridge county, Va, until 1737)

The maiden name of Mary Dean's mother was Jane McAllister, who was one of the heroic women who aided in the successful defense of Londonderry in the great siege by James II, in 1690.   At the close of the War of the Revolution, Abram Irvine removed with his family from Rockbridge county, Va, to Kentucky, and settled in what afterwards became first the county of Mercer,

and subsequently and now the county of Boyle, on the waters of Salt river,
about five miles southwest of the present town of Danville A few miles to
the east, Isaac Shelby, who afterwards became the first governor of Kentucky,
settled, and the places of Abram Irvine and Shelby are both noted on the first
map of Kentucky, made, I think, in 1786, by John Filson.

Abram Irvine and Mary Dean had eleven children, nine of whom married
and reared families of children. These children and their descendants are as
follows

1 JOHN IRVINE, born February 25, 1755, married Prudence Armstrong,
of Mercer county, Kentucky He was one of the magistrates who held
the first county court in Mercer county while it was still a part of Virginia.
This was in August, 1786, and associated with him were Samuel McDowell
and Gabriel Madison The children of John and Prudence Armstrong
Irvine were

   1 Samuel, who married, first, Cassy Briscoe and by her had three
   children (a) Rev. John, who married Matilda Smith, (b) Jeremiah Briscoe, and (c) William, who married Eliza Mann, and,
   second, Elizabeth Adams, by whom he had two children, Mary,
   who married James Forsythe, and David

   2 Mary, who married Dr. James McElroy, and by him had three
   children (a) Alice, who married a Norton in Marion county, Mo,
   (b) Dr Irvine, who married, also, in Marion county, Mo., and
   (c) Milton, who never married They all lived in Missouri

   3 Margaret, who married Dr David Clarke, who, with their family,
   also lived in Missouri, chiefly in Marion county Their children
   were (a) Robert, who died unmarried, (b) Margaret, who married a Dr Gore, and (c) Josephine, who married a Hatcher

   4 Sarah, who married Horace Clelland, of Lebanon Their children
   were (a) Elizabeth, who married a Dr Walker, (b) John, who
   died unmarried, and (c) Rev Thomas H , who was married three
   times, his third wife was Sally Ray

   5 Abram, who married Amelia Templeton Their children were
   (a) Leonidas, who married Bell Burton, (b) Lucy, who married
   Rev Robert Caldwell, (c) Ellen P , who married Joseph Mc-
   Dowell, a grandson of Col Joseph McDowell and Sarah Irvine,
   daughter of Abram and Mary Dean Irvine, (d) Joseph W , who
   married, first, Mariah Brumfield, and second, Mary Davis, of
   Bloomfield, Ky , (e) Margaret C , who married Anthony McElroy,
   of Springfield, (f) Gabriel C , who was married three times, his
   first wife being Elizabeth Gregory, and his second being her
   sister, his third wife was a Miss Hughes, (g) Abram P , who
   married Elizabeth Fleece

   6 Priscilla, who married Dr M S Shuck, of Lebanon Their

children were, (a) Mary, who married Charles R McElroy, of
Springfield, (b) John Irvine, who married Mary Young, and
(c) Solomon S

7 Robert   I do not know the names of his wife and children

II HANS, born April 25, 1758   He was never married

III MARY, married, first, William Adair, by whom she had two children (1)
Alexander, who married Elizabeth Monroe, by whom he had six children,
(a) Anna, who married Dr Lewis of Greensburg, Ky, (b) Mary, who
married Thomas Wagner, of Greensburg, (c) Kate, who married Gen E
H Hobson, of Greensburg, (d) Monroe, (e) John, and (f) William.
Her second husband was Dr Issachar Paulding, by whom she had no
children

IV MARGARET, born April 25, 1762, married, first, Samuel Lapsley, and
second, Rev John Lyle, the first Presbyterian preacher in Kentucky, by
whom she had the following children

    1 Sarah, whose first husband was Rev Joseph B Lapsley, by whom
      she had two children, (a) Samuel, who married Mary Jane
      Bronaugh, and resided at Lincoln, Mo, and (b) Margaret, who
      married John Taylor, of Missouri   Her second husband was a
      Witherspoon, of Missouri   I do not know their children. This
      family all lived in Missouri

    2 John R , who married his cousin, Sarah Irvine, daughter of Robert
      and Judith Glover Irvine   Their children were (a) William J ,
      who married his cousin, Ellen Lyle, of Paris, (b) Robert B , who
      married Mary McElroy, of Lebanon; and (c) Edwin, who died
      unmarried after reaching maturity   There were other children
      but they died early

    3 Abram Irvine, who married Frances Hunly, by whom he had two
      children (a) John Andrew, who married Belle Russell, (b) Joel
      Irvine, who married, first, Emma Railey, and second, Cornelia
      Railey

V ANNE, born November 28, 1763, who married her cousin, Samuel
McDowell, born March 8, 1764, who was a youthful soldier of the Revolutionary War   They had the following children

    1. Mary, who married William Starling   Their children were (a)
      General Lyne, of the Union army, who married Marie Antoinette
      Hensley, (b) Colonel Samuel, also of the Union army, who
      married Elizabeth Lewis, and (c) Col. Edmund Alexander, also
      of the Union army, who married Anna L McCarroll, of Hop-
      kinsville

    2. John Adair, who married Lucy Todd Starling, and removed to
      Columbus, Ohio, where he afterwards became a judge, but died
      at thirty four years of age   Their children were (a) Anna

Irvine, who married Judge John Winston Price, of Hillsboro,
Ohio, (b) Starling, who died young, (c) Jane, who married John
A Smith, of Hillsboro, and (d) William, who never married

3 Abram Irvine, who married Eliza Selden Lord   He resided at
Columbus, and was clerk of the Supreme Court of Ohio for many
years   Their children were   (a) Gen Irvine McDowell, who
commanded the United States army at Bull Run   He married a
Miss Burden, of Troy, N Y , (b) Anna, who married a Massey,
formerly of Virginia, but afterwards of Memphis, Tenn , (c) John,
who was a colonel in the Union army, (d) Eloise, who married a
Colonel Bridgeman, of the United States army, and (e) Malcolm,
who married Jane Gordon, and resided in Cincinnati

4 Wm Adair, who married Mariah Hawkins Harvey, of Virginia
He was a physician and resided in Louisville   Their children
were (a) Sarah Shelby, who married Judge Bland Ballard, of
Louisville, (b) Henry Clay, who married Annette Clay, granddaughter of Henry Clay, and daughter of Lieut-Col Henry
Clay, who was killed at Buena Vista   They reside at "Ashland," the old Clay homestead, near Lexington, (c) Anna, (d)
Magdalen; (e) William Preston, who married Katherine Wright,
and resides in Louisville, and (f) Edward Irvine, who was a
soldier in the Union army and was killed at Resaca   He was
never married

5 Joseph, who married Anne Bush, and settled in Alabama   Their
children were   (a) Mary, who married Judge Clarke, of Mississippi, and (b) Elizabeth, who married Dr Welch, and settled in
Galveston, Texas

6 Sarah, who married Jeremiah Minter, of Columbus   Their children were   (a) Ann, who married Alonzo Slayback, of Missouri,
(b) McDowell, who never married, (c) Magdaline, who married a
Kidd, of Illinois, (d) Mariah, who married a Colorado man,
whose name I do not know, (e) Bertrude, who died in the Union
army during the war, unmarried, (f) Ellen, and (g) Susan. I
do not know whom they married   Nearly all of this family and
their descendants live in Missouri.

7. Reed

8 Alexander, who married, first, Priscilla McAfee, daughter of Gen
Robert McAfee, who had removed from Mercer county to
Missouri. She, with her only child, perished in the burning of
a steamboat on the Mississippi river   His second wife was Anna
Haupt, of Mississippi   Their children were   (a) Louise Irvine,
who married her cousin, Dr. Hervy McDowell, of Cynthiana,
and (b) Anna, who never married

VI ABRAM, born August 8, 1766, married, first, Sally Henry, a relative of Patrick Henry, and second, Margaret McAfee By his first wife he had only one child, Jane, who married Lee M Speak Their children were (*a*) Frank, who married Mary Hunter, (*b*) Magdalen, who married James McKee, and removed to Texas, (*c*) Sarah, who married Rev J. I. McKee, D. D , vice-president of Centre College, (*d*) Jane, who married Dr William Mourning, of Springfield, (*e*) Julia, who married Castello Barfield, of Tennessee, (*f*) Emine, who married John Mitchell, of Missouri, and (*g*) Irvine, who died unmarried The children of Abram Irvine and Margaret McAfee were

   1 James H , who married Elizabeth Williamson. Their children were. (*a*) John Williamson, who married Anna Simpson, of Indiana, he resides in Missouri, (*b*) Anna Bella, who never married, (*c*) Elizabeth, who never married, and (*d*) Cornelia Crittenden, who married her cousin, Joseph McDowell Wallace, and resides at Danville.

   2 Abram Lyle, who married Sarah Hughes Their only child was Letitia Reed, who married Capt A M Burbank They reside in Atlanta

   3 Issachar Paulding, who married Margaret Muldrough Their only children, Hugh and Letitia, died unmarried

   4 Elizabeth, who married Anselm D Meyer Their children were (*a*) Ardis Rebecca, who married Thomas R. Browne, of Washington county, (*b*) Margaret C., who married Stephen E. Browne, and removed to Missouri; (*c*) James, who died unmarried, (*d*) John Miller, who married Fanny English, (*e*) Edward Hopkins, who married Alice Mann, of Mercer, and (*f*) Mary Irvine, who never married.

   5 Mary Paulding, who married her cousin, Abram Dean Irvine, son of Robert Irvine and Judith Glover Their children were (*a*) Abram Walter, who married Sophia Tate, of Taylor county (these were my parents), (*b*) Elizabeth M , who married Rev. L. H Blanton, D D , chancellor of Central University, (*c*) Robert Lyle, who married Anna Seymour, of Chillicothe, Ohio, to which place he removed, (*d*) Mary Paulding, who was never married, and (*e*) Rev William, who married Elizabeth Lacy Hoge, of Richmond, Va There were several other children who died young and unmarried, their names were: Margaret Sarah, Judith Glover, John, and Sally Lyle.

VII. ROBERT, born 1768, married Judith Glover. Their children were.

   1 John Glover, who married Emiline Drake Their children were (*a*) William Drake, who married Corilla Parker, of Fayette county, and (*b*) Emeline, who died unmarried

2 Abram Dean, who married his cousin, Mary Paulding Irvine, whose children I have enumerated above

3 Robert, who married Ann Armstrong. Their children were (*a*) Robert Andrew, who married Mattie Logan, of Shelby county, (*b*) Judith Emma, who married Rev. William Cooper

4. Mary who married, first, Walter Prather. Their children were (*a*) Martha, who married, first, a Caps, and second, a Cunningham (*b*) Mary, who married, first, Nineon Prather, second, Thomas Rickets and third, Samuel Varble, (*c*) William, who married Susan Blackwell, (*d*) Robert, who married Martha Johnson, (*e*) Walter, who married Mary Prather, (*f*) Irvine, who married Sarah Peyton, and (*g*) Sarah, who married Benjamin Baker   The second husband of Mary Irvine was a Shrock, by whom she had one child, Edward, who married Laura Taylor

5 Judith, who married a Brink   They had no children

6 Celia, who married William Davenport. They had only one child, Judith, who married, first, George St Clair, and second, John Sparks

7. Sarah, who married her cousin, John R Lyle, whose children I have already given

VIII NANCY, born July 5, 1770, married Francis McMordie. Their children were

1 Abram Irvine, who married, first, Jane Armstrong, and by her had one child, Francis, who died, a Confederate soldier, during the war, and unmarried, second, Jane Hurt, by whom he had the following children   (*a*) Nancy, who married Samuel Lackey and removed to Texas, (*b*) Mary, who died without issue, (*c*) Magdalen, who married Elijah Vanarsdale, of Mercer, (*d*) Abram Irvine, who married Nancy Harris, of Mercer.

2 Mary, who married William Cowan. Their children were (*a*) John, who never married, he died in Cuba, (*b*) Nancy, who married Rev. John Bogle, (*c*) Sarah, who married William Harrison, (*d*) Robert, who was a Confederate officer, and was killed in the battle of Green River Bridge, unmarried, (*e*) Jane, who married Rev Geo O Barnes, (*f*) Dr Francis, who died in the City of Mexico, unmarried, (*g*) James, a Confederate soldier, and (*h*) Abram Irvine   The last two went to Colorado, I do not know about their descendants.

3 Margaret, married, I think, James Crawford, of South Carolina   I do not know about their children, if any   Nancy Irvine and Francis McMurdie had three other children — Robert, Jane and Hans, but I think they all died unmarried and without issue.

IX ELIZABETH, born March 20, 1772, married George Caldwell Their children were

    1 Abram Irvine, who married his cousin, Anne McDowell Their children were (a) Belle, who died unmarried; (b) William, who married Callie Adams, (c) Elizabeth, who married Preston Talbott, (d) Anne, who married John Yeiser, (e) Irvine, who died unmarried, (f) Caleb, who married Lou Woolfork, and (g) Cowan, who married John C Crawford, of Texas.

    2 Isabella, who married Benjamin Perkins Their children were (a) Mary, who married Nicholas Bowman, and (b) George, who never married

    3 Dr John, who married Jane Fox. Their children were (a) Mary, who married Cyrus Richardson, (b) Amanda, (c) Belle, neither of whom was ever married, and (d) Sophia, who married Dr Parker, of Somerset, Ky There were three other children of Elizabeth Irvine and George Caldwell, George, Mary and Eliza, but I think none of them married, or left descendants

X SARAH, born November 21, 1774; married her cousin, Col Joseph McDowell, a brother of Judge Samuel McDowell, who married Anna Irvine, the elder sister of Sarah Their children were

    1 Samuel, who married, first, Mariah Ball, they had only one child, Mary, who married Dr J M Meyer His second wife was Martha Hawkins, and their children were (a) Joseph, who married his cousin, Ellen Irvine, whom I have mentioned before, (b) Charles, (c) Nicholas, who married Elizabeth McElroy, of Springfield, (d) Samuel, who married Mattie McElroy, sister of Elizabeth, (e) William, who died unmarried

    2. Anne, who married her cousin, Abram I Caldwell, and whose children have already been given

    3. Sarah, who married Michael Sullivant, of Columbus, Ohio, afterwards Illinois Their children were (a) Anna, who married E L. Davidson, of Springfield, Ky, (b) Sallie, (c) Joseph McDowell, of Illinois, (d) Lou, who married William Hopkins, of Henderson, Ky

    4 Margaret, who married Joseph Sullivant, brother of Michael, their only child was Margaret Irvine, who married Gen Henry B Carrington, of the United States army

    5. Lucy, who died unmarried

    6 Charles, who died unmarried

    7 Caleb, who died unmarried

    8 Magdalen, who married Caleb Wallace, of Danville She survives him, with two sons, (a) Joseph McDowell, who married his cousin, Cornelia C Irvine before mentioned, and (b) Woodford

XI WILLIAM DEAN, born August 1775 (?); never married He was an
officer in the War of 1812, and subsequently died at Natchez, Miss

In this I have attempted merely to give you a list of the descendants of
Abram Irvine and Mary Dean to the third generation. It is a mere skele-
ton. To fill in, to give life and flesh, dates of birth and death, collateral marriage connections, the occupations, the achievements and leading characteristics
of all who are worthy of special mention would require a volume It is a
noble line—pure Scotch-Irish, the blood that has done more than any other to
turn the American wilderness into the strongest and most enlightened nation
the world has yet known   We shall search history in vain, I think, for a
family that combines in a higher degree love of God, of kindred and country,
with the highest personal integrity, dauntless will, energy of purpose, and a
burning devotion to liberty in all its forms, that could have been nourished
nowhere else than among the intrepid clans that followed Wallace and Bruce
to battle

My chief objection to our great composite national life is that the members of our best families are too prone to become absorbed in the general
hurlyburly, and to forget their past   This is to lose the greatest of all stimu-
lants to lofty purpose and unceasing exertion   The noble work you are doing
will do much, very much, to recall us of the present, and the generations yet
unborn, to realize the debt we owe to heredity, and to incite us to new
resolves to meet that responsibility

Elizabeth Irvine.

Since this story was told me an immeasurable desert of buried years,
haunted by the ghosts of departed hopes, stretches between me and the distant time I listened to it, and I can hardly realize that I and the child who wept
over the fate of fair Elizabeth Irvine are one and the same person

The name of Elizabeth Irvine's father—other than Irvine—I know not,
but this I heard. that he was a Scotch-Irishman, of a noble family, and that
he came to this country and married a beautiful French woman, who could not
speak English well, and who brought great wealth to her husband on her marriage day.

Elizabeth Irvine was born in the South   Why I have always thought that
she was born near New Orleans I do not know, but such an impression has been
borne in on my mind ever since I heard her story, now more years ago than I
care to count

Elizabeth inherited her mother's beauty and her father's intellect, which was
said to have been considerable , and to these rare possessions had been added,
by the time Elizabeth had reached her eighteenth birthday, a good education

She had been graduated in some large city in the East, but, if I ever heard the name of it, it does not dwell in my memory

In the town—or city, as I think it was—where Elizabeth Irvine was born there lived a certain wealthy and distinguished judge, whom I shall call Judge S , for fear, if I should be more particular, I might offend some one now living who might be nearly related to him. His direct descendant he could not be, for, although the judge married, he drew a blank in the infant lottery, and no child ever called him father,

Judge S was forty years old the first time he and Elizabeth met, after her return from school , but he was not bald or gray and was eminently handsome and attractive Judge S had been the schoolmate and friend of Mr Irvine, although Mr. Irvine was a few years his senior. He was often invited to Mr Irvine's house, and often took the liberty of a life-long friend to call when he was not invited In this way he saw a great deal of Elizabeth, and no one was surprised when he asked her to be his wife — not even Elizabeth, although she promptly, but kindly, refused to marry him She took the sting from her refusal by saying that she intended to see the world before she entered into so solemn and responsible a compact as marriage, and that the judge must give her time to look about her The judge did not feel hopeless about finally winning Elizabeth, because there was no rival in view, even if Elizabeth did have a vast deal of attention from the young men of her acquaintance

But there was a rival coming from an obscure corner of a distant State, and one whom the judge, if he had only known, might have dreaded through his whole life.

One morning, as the judge sat in the morning room of his stately mansion, there came a ring at the door-bell, and a young man just from a long journey stood before him At the first glance the judge, who was well versed in human nature, knew that the youth before him was no ordinary character, for, beside being handsome, his bearing was that of an educated gentleman , and the judge arose, gave his name and offered the young man a chair. The young man gave his own name, thanked the judge, and seated himself I shall call this young man James Allen, although that was not his name, nor anything like it, but it will serve my purpose in this story as well as another name and much better than the one he afterwards made famous, and which he had legally inherited from his father

Judge S. took this young man to board in his house and gave him the use of his law books and his office, and in a year after Mr. Allen's first appearance in Judge S 's presence he was admitted to the bar and had won golden opinions from many of the older lawyers, and had stolen the heart of Elizabeth Irvine, who, it seemed, had had time to take a look about her and to see the world, for she was willing to enter into the solemn and responsible compact of marriage with Mr Allen, if he a- ld g- - - - - before it should be solemnized by law

4

and the church. Elizabeth's mother was a Catholic of the Roman persuasion, and her father was a Presbyterian, but neither of them was of the strictest sect, for they never had discussions on their different faiths, but went their several ways in quietness and peace and often went to the Presbyterian church together, and as often sat side by side while the old priest held forth, before the altar, of the only way to Heaven   Thus Elizabeth, hearing much doctrinal truth, and having as much love for and faith in one parent as she had in the other, sought out a way to save her own soul, as also a means in so doing of offending neither parent, and she became an Episcopalian   She had been baptized when she was a few weeks old, so it only remained that she be confirmed in the church of her choice   Her father and mother both attended her at her confirmation, and afterward they went with their only and beloved child to her church, and she went to theirs and still there were no religious disputes, nor were any fears expressed that any member of that family of three souls was in danger of— shall I say hell-fire ? Preachers used to rip out that expression in my youth, and although I shuddered at it, it made me afraid to do wrong, so I shall let it stand

Mr Allen besought Elizabeth more than once to shorten his probation and name an earlier day for their wedding, but she held firmly to the first arrangement, and Mr Allen was forced to wait for the blessings in store for him and the time when he should call Elizabeth his wife and be enabled to bask, from day to day, in the light of her gracious presence

Those two, Elizabeth and James Allen, were betrothed one June evening, in what year I am sorry I can not tell, and Mr Allen said, as he placed the ring on Elizabeth's finger, "This day one year I shall replace this ring with another, and then you will be mine, Elizabeth, through time and eternity "

How much sorrow and misfortune can gather and fall in twelve months! Six months after this date Elizabeth's mother sickened and died, and before the year was out her father slept beside her   At his death it was learned that security debts would sweep away his whole estate   Elizabeth was left not only alone, but almost penniless

She begged Mr Allen to postpone their marriage, and he, in his sorrow for his beloved, did so, and Elizabeth went East to the school in which she had been educated, and remained there until within a few weeks of the time appointed for her marriage to take place   An old friend, who had loved her father and mother and who had loved Elizabeth from her infancy, had written Elizabeth to beg that she should be married from her house

This friend lived in sight of Mr Irvine's old home, now in the possession of strangers, and when Elizabeth came to stay with her, to wait for the appointed time that was to make her and Mr Allen one, she thought that the change she saw in Elizabeth was due to grief and sorrow at beholding the pleasant home that was hers no longer

When Judge S called to see Elizabeth he could not understand the manner of the w   h   ill h   t, b   k n c ment   n l h d y came on

for which Mr Allen had waited so impatiently, and he and Elizabeth stood before the altar to be made man and wife

Judge S was to give the bride away Just as the clergyman had opened his lips to begin the service Elizabeth fainted, or, they said, pretended to faint, and a second time the wedding was postponed, this time indefinitely.

Mr Allen had an interview with Elizabeth on the evening of the day on which he had hoped to have claimed her for his own What passed between them was never known, but it must have had a stormy termination, for he left town that night When Elizabeth arose from her bed of illness her friends noticed that she no longer wore her engagement ring, but on this subject she was silent as the grave, and none dared question her

Months went by—six of them—and still Mr Allen did not return Judge S again renewed his attentions to Elizabeth, and with greater success than formerly, for she not only agreed to marry him, but appointed an early day for their nuptials

Just before her wedding day Mr Allen returned. He was present and heard her promise, in a clear, distinct voice, to honor and obey Judge S , but he and others noticed that, if she promised to love him, she must have done so in an undertone, for she could not be heard

Judge S entered into partnership with Mr Allen, and the latter boarded with the judge as he had done before the marriage, but Mrs Grundy noticed that he never went to his meals nor near Judge S 's house in the judge's absence Another thing Mrs Grundy took note of Elizabeth was growing thin and pale She was always most gentle and considerate in her manner to Judge S , and acted as if she had done him a great wrong and wished, in some way, to make atonement for it

She had not been married very long, when her husband was elected to Congress As he was elected some time during President Jackson's administration, I come to the only date I have yet been able to furnish He removed to Washington, with his wife, some time between the years 1829 and 1837

Elizabeth seemed to regain her wonted appearance and spirits in the Capital, which was said to have been very gay at that time

Elizabeth was very much admired and was entertained by, and she and her husband entertained, all the dignitaries who were assembled at Washington from this country and abroad There never was a whisper against Elizabeth's fair fame, although Andrew Jackson was President of the United States, and held his court to please himself, and made and unmade his cabinet without regard to the murmurs and complaints that came from all over the country

I never heard that Judge S s wife did or did not meet Andrew Jackson, but this I have heard, which I shall never forget, Elizabeth became a consummate politician and wrote learned articles on the vexed issues of the day and made herself famous by being the author of the " Jackson Letters, so-called because th

Although magazines and newspapers are the evangels of civilization and progress, nothing is so evanescent as the fame of those who write for them. "The Jackson Letters" are lost   I may be the only one now living who ever heard of them and the only soul on earth who knows the story of fair Elizabeth Irvine

She died in Wahington, D C , and her broken-hearted husband took her body to the place of her nativity

> " Among familiar scenes to rest,
> And in the places of her youth "

On her death-bed she said to one, who told me her story, " If ' the wages of sin is death,' the wages of ambition are ashes and dust

" Bury me in my wedding gown   I have kept it for that purpose, but I did not think to need it so soon   Comfort my husband when I am gone   I have tried to be faithful to him, but when I am in the grave none will ever know how sad a heart death has stilled "

One must have suspected, for, at nightfall on the day Elizabeth was laid to rest by her mother and father, a man who lived near the graveyard saw James Allen climb the crumbling stone wall that enclosed the churchyard and make his way to Elizabeth's grave, and he saw him leave it the next morning before sunrise

Mr. Allen lived to the verge of extreme old age, but he never married. His name is well known to American people for he became famous.

Thus endeth a lesson that will not teach

Threnody.

Along the far horizon's verge the smoldering sundown burns,
The sky, above its dying light, to opal softness turns
Now, ghostly, by each vale and stream the mists and shadows creep,
While, in the faded autumn trees, birds hush their young to sleep,
And whispering winds, from other lands, pass softly on their way,
As twilight weaves a purple shroud for the departed day,
While on the hilltop's line of light, etched on the fading sky,
The gentle kine are standing, mute, to watch the daylight die

How many years before I lived the sun shone down you vale,
And on this path, where lovers walked, to tell that endless tale '
Then other birds, in other trees, sang out their tuneful lay,
And other hearts, as sad as mine, beat out their little day
Here, long ago, some gentle maid has watched the evening star
Lead all the hosts of heaven to light the deeps of night afar ,
Then turned to watch the harvest moon climb o'er the eastern hill
While the twin phantoms, Love and Hope, her heart with rapture fill
Alas ' why did she come to earth so short a time to stay
And where now is her gentle soul among the stars to-day

I call to where the millions sleep, within their moldy beds,
And where, beneath a starless sky eternal darkness spreads
The sages turn within the dust, and murmur in their sleep
" The keys of life and death are hid in mystery's dungeon deep
Man lives and loves, he toils and weeps, then lies so cold and still,
Forgetting, in his narrow bed, how once his heart could thrill,
And he who followed duty s path and he who won renown,
Have somewhere in the narrow vale laid all their burdens down
And she who drained dark sorrow's grail is calm and peaceful now,
Since death s impartial touch has smoothed care's lines from cheek and brow
The wherefore is forever hid till suns shall cease to set—
Then murmur not that life should mean to love and to forget'"

Cynthiana Ky , September 29, 1897   *L. Ford*

ISAIAH TUCKER IRVIN, married, 1840, Miss Elizabeth Joyner, daughter
of William Howlett Joyner, of Beaufort county, South Carolina Their
children are five sons and three daughters, viz

1 Sarah Joyner, married, 1863, James Hillhouse Alexander, son of
Adam L Alexander, who was a prominent and honored citizen
of Washington, Ga , and who reared a family of ten children,
widely known and respected throughout Georgia Their children
are two sons and one daughter, viz (a) Irvin, attorney at law,
Atlanta, Ga , unmarried, (b) Hugh H , married, 1891, Miss Mary
Burton, daughter of Thos J Burton, a large planter, of Burke
county, Georgia They have one daughter, Louisa Porter, born
1893 , (c) Elizabeth, married, 1894, Mr Llewellyn G Doughty, son
of Dr Wm H Doughty, a distinguished physician of Augusta
Ga. They have one daughter, Jean Irvine, born 1896

2. William Howlett, married, 1867 Miss Hattie Callaway, daughter
of Wm R Callaway, of Wilkes county, Georgia, and granddaughter of the celebrated pioneer Baptist preacher of Middle
Georgia, Enoch Callaway They have ten living children, five
sons and five daughters (a) Claude, unmarried, went to the West
about 1890, (b) William Howlett, Jr , married in 1894, and has
two children, (c) Elizabeth J , married, 1896, William Martin, a
farmer of Oglethorpe county Georgia, (d) Sarah Alexander,
(e) Charles Edgar, (f) Annie May, (g) Isaiah Tucker,
(h) Everett, (j) Willie Rosa, (k) Hattie

3 Charles Edgar, married Miss Mary Fortson, daughter of Benjamin
W Fortson, a prominent citizen of Wilkes county, Ga Their
children are (a) Isaiah Tucker, (b) Reba, (c) Alexander,
(d) Mary, (e) Emma

4 Jean Isabella, married Major Norman W. Smith, of Augusta, Ga ,
a wealthy man but ... and had two children ... live in the

Quartermaster's Department of the Confederate Army   They
have no children

5 Benjamin Screven, married, first, Miss Sallie Hill, of the large and
distinguished family of that name in Wilkes county, Georgia, by
whom he has one son, Paul, and, secondly, Miss Browne Brewer,
of a prominent and cultured family, of Hayneville, Ala , by whom
he has one infant daughter, Mildred

6. Isaiah Tucker, married (1874), Miss Elizabeth Willis, daughter of
James H Willis, a distinguished, public-spirited citizen of Wilkes
county, Georgia   Their children are four, viz (*a*) Sarah
Elizabeth , (*b*) Leila , (*c*) Benjamin S , (*d*) Willis

7 Barnett, married (1892), Miss Ruth Foreman, daughter of Rufus
L Foreman, merchant and farmer, of Washington, Wilkes
county, Georgia

8 Mary Bowdie, married George Twiggs Bryan, son of Gen Goode
Bryan, who was distinguished in the Flordia War, and a Brigadier-
General in the Confederate Army   She died in 1892, leaving one
daughter, Anna Twiggs Bryan

Mr Isaiah T Irvin, the father of this family of eight children was prominent as a lawyer and an official, being Speaker of the Georgia House of Representatives at the period of his untimely death   He lost his life in a steamboat
explosion, in 1860, while traveling in Texas, on the Buffalo Bayou, near
Houston   His wife, Mrs Elizabeth Joyner Irvin, died in Augusta, Georgia,
in 1891, at the home of her daughter, Mrs. Alexander.

One of the finest military companies that entered the Confederate service
from Georgia was the Irvin Guard, organized by Isaiah T Irvin, in 1860, of
which he had been commissioned captain just prior to his death   His son,
Charles E Irvin, aged then about sixteen, entered the service in this company,
as a private, and before the close of the war had become its captain, serving
with marked efficiency and gallantry throughout the Confederate War   All the
males of the family and connections over fifteen years of age served with the
Confederate Army.

My grandfather (James Callaway's grandfather) Christopher Irvine, en-
listed in the Fifth Virginia Regiment February 15, 1776. He married Louisa
Tucker, by whom he had two sons, Charles and Isaiah Tucker   He moved to
Georgia when these boys were small (I do not know what year), settled in
Wilkes county, and married a second time   By his second wife he had two
children—one son, Judge David Irvine, of Marietta, Ga , and one daughter,
Lucinda, dead

My father, Isaiah Tucker, son of Christopher Irvine, married Isabelle
Barkston and settled in Wilkes county, Georgia   They lived together in the
same place fifty-three years   Father died at the age of seventy-three, mother
ninety-one   He recorded a large plantation country-tone, black-

smith shop and public gin   Carried his cotton to Augusta, Ga , the nearest market, 100 miles away, on wagons   They had eight children—two sons, Charles and Isaiah Tucker, and six daughters, Louisa, Nancy, Lucinda, Prudence, Mary, and Martha.   All were Christian people and joined the Baptist church, except Isaiah Tucker, who joined the Methodist, were baptized at Sardis, by Enoch Callaway and Jesse Mercer

Charles Irvine, son of Isaiah Tucker, son of Christopher Irvine, married Harriet Battle, and had two children, Charles B Irvine, of Atlanta, Ga , and Mary Bell (Mrs M B Wharton, of Norfolk, Va)

Isaiah Tucker, son of Isaiah Tucker, son of Christopher Irvine, married Elizabeth Joyner, and had eight children—five sons, Howlett, Charles, Benjamin, Isaiah Tucker, Barnett, and three daughters, Sallie (Mrs James H. Alexander, of Augusta, Ga), Janie (Mis Norman W Smith, of Augusta, Ga), Mamie (Mrs Geo T. Bryan, dead)

Louisa, daughter of Isaiah Tucker, son of Christopher Irvine, married, first, Lewis Davis, and had six children , second, Baylis Crosby, and had five children

Nancy, daughter of Isaiah Tucker, son of Christopher Irvine, married Thomas Favor, and had seven children

Prudence, daughter of Isaiah Tucker, son of Christopher Irvine married, first, John P Johnson, and had one child , second, Iverson L Brooks, and had two children

Mary, daughter of Isaiah Tucker, son of Christopher Irvine, married John Walton, three children   Afterwards married Merrell Calloway , four children

Martha, daughter of Isaiah Tucker, son of Christopher Irvine, married Oliver L Battle.   They had five children—two sons, Charles and John Tucker, and three daughters, Eliza, Mary Belle and Annie Porter

Charles Battle, son of Martha (great-grandson of Christopher Irvine), married Lou Walker

John T son of Martha (great-grandson of Christopher Irvine), married Rosalie Waddey They had three children, Oliver I , Waddey W and Mary Belle

Eliza, daughter of Martha, and great-granddaughter of Christopher Irvine, married John F Ficklen   They had two children, John Fielding and Irvine

Mary Belle, daughter of Martha, and great-granddaughter of Christopher Irvine, married John F. Ficklen

Anna Porter, daughter of Martha and great-granddaughter of Christopher Irvine, married Wm Howell Wood, and had one child, Mary Belle

MARTHA IRVINE BAILIF

I am requested by my cousin, Mrs M B Wharton, of Norfolk, Va , to send you a few items of the history of my father and his family   My father, David Irwin, or Irvin or Irvine, I don't know exactly which, as some of them spell it the two last-named ways and some is my father did Irwin though we

know we are closely related   The two first of the name that I have any history
of were William and John, who came. I think, to Philadelphia from Ireland
William Irwin had a son named Christopher, who went to Virginia and from
there to Wilkes county, Georgia, where he married a Miss Tucker, by whom
he had two sons, Isaiah Tucker and Charles   His wife died and he married
Prudence Echols, by whom he had Christopher, Jr., William, John, Smith,
Heflin, and a daughter, Catherine, and the youngest child was a son, David, who
was my father, he married Sarah Royston, from which union the following
children were born   Marcus J , died, aged twenty-three years , Mary Elizabeth,
died, aged seven years , Margaret Isabella, who married George N. Lester, who
was Attorney-General at his death, in 1892, and his wife, Margaret, died the
same year, leaving five sons and two daughters, viz   Mary I Lester, David P
Lester, Joseph II. Lester, Geo. N Lester, Jr , Sarah Lester, Irwin Lester and
Robert T Lester   Next was Julia Irwin, who married Greenlee Butler, who
died in 1864 leaving her a widow , next is Maria E , who is unmarried ; next,
Robert C , who is an attache of the Comptroller-General's office of Georgia (I
should have said insurance clerk), next, David, Jr , who died in 1856, aged ten
years , next, Thomas B , who is a lawyer in Marietta, Ga

My wife was Miss Mary Lane, and Thomas B married Miss Lilla Atkinson, granddaughter of ex-Governor Chas J McDonald, deceased. My father,
David Irwin, obtained, by his own untiring efforts, a fine education, by energy
succeeding in getting sufficient education to study the legal profession, and was
for a number of years a judge of the Superior Court   He was elected by the
Legislature, with two others, to compile the first Code of Georgia, and afterward
appointed to revise it, alone   During the days of Reconstruction he was nominated by the Democratic party for Governor, but, Georgia being under military
rule, he was informed by General Meade, who was in command of this department, that he would not be allowed to take his seat, if elected, which his
friends thought was a foregone conclusion, as all the leading Republicans were
supporting him, as well as the Democrats   His opponent was Rufus E Bullock.   My father declined the race, and General Gordon was put up and
defeated by Governor Bullock   The reason General Meade gave was that my
father had been an elector for Jefferson Davis when he was a candidate for
President, but the true reason was that a faction got the General to give
this opinion to get my father out of the race, because he had been an
old Whig and was carrying the Republican party for that reason, and they
thought he might be too good a friend to those of that party who supported
him   He was a self-made man, as his father died when he was a few years
old, leaving his mother but little of this world's goods, and, though he was
the youngest child, she had to depend on him more than on any of the others

The first named John, I think, is the founder of the western branch of the
family, many of whom are in Mississippi, Tennessee and Illinois   My father
was related to the Adams, of Virginia, and also the McDowells. I think, of

Pennsylvania, but I don't know the relationship. He died in 1885, at the age of seventy-eight.

Please excuse this hurried sketch, as I had to get it up from memory, and give it in a disjointed manner. Very truly,

R. C. IRWIN.

P. S.—I forgot to give names of children of R. C. The children of Robt. C. Irwin and Mary W. Lane are Julia Greenlee, Mark A., Sarah, Hope (a boy), Lucy Mary and Margaret I. Sarah and Margaret I. died when young. The children of Thos. B. Irwin and Lilla Atkinson are David, Mary Ann, Alexander A. and George L.

Descendants of Gen. Robert Irvine.

General Robert Irvine, who married Mary Alexander, was one of the signers of the Mecklenburg "Declaration of Independence." General Robert Irvine lived in Charlotte, N. C.

Margaret Irvine, daughter of General Robert Irvine, was married to Hugh McDowell, of Mecklenburg county, North Carolina. Hugh McDowell was the son of John McDowell of Revolutionary fame. Margaret McDowell, daughter of Hugh McDowell and Margaret Irvine his wife, married Andrew Lawson Barry, of South Carolina, son of John Barry and grandson of Capt. Andrew Barry, celebrated at the battle of Cowpens.

The issue of the marriage between Margaret McDowell and Andrew Lawson Barry was as follows: Euphemia Elizabeth, Robert Lindsay, Mary Jane and Sarah Ann.

Euphemia Elizabeth married William Adolphus Moore, issue: Emma Eliza, Sallie Irvine, who died in 1875, Susan Margaret, who died in childhood, Mary Lou, who died in 1881, William Andrew, who died in childhood, Anna Euphemia, John McDowell, Jessie and Wilmer Lee.

Emma Eliza married William Wood Draper of Alabama, issue: William Moore, Robert Daniel, Mary Emma, Bessie, Jesse H., and Wallace Wood.

Anna Euphemia married Seaborne Wright, of Rome, Ga., issue: Thomas Barry, Louis Moore, Max, Seaborne, who died in infancy, and Graham.

John McDowell Moore married Hattie Grace Wharton, issue: Wharton Adolphus, Elizabeth Irvine, May Bell, Emma, who died in infancy, and Bertha Hardon.

Jessie Moore married Hugh L. McKee, issue: Jessie Moore and Margaret Moore.

Wilmer Lee Moore married Cornelia Jackson, issue: Cornelia Jackson.

Descendants of the House of Bonshaw--Irish Branch.

Hugh McDowell, of Mecklenburg, N C , son of John McDowell of Revolutionary fame, married Margaret Irvin, daughter of Gen Robert Irvine, one of the signers of the Mecklenburg Declaration of Independence

Sarah Salina, daughter of Hugh and Margaret McDowell, married Andrew Moore Sloan, of South Carolina, issue John Hugh, Charles Andrew, Oscar Adam and Robert Eugene

John Hugh married Mary C Winn, of Thomasville, Ga , issue Johnnie Hugh

Johnnie Hugh married Edward Buickley, of Manistee, Mich , issue Virginia

Charles Andrew married Mollie L Morris, of Monticello, Fla issue Emma.

Oscar Adam married Elizabeth Irwin Sloan, of McDonough, Ga , issue Sarah Eva, Annie May and Andrew Moore.

Robert Eugene married Ida Turnbull, of Monticello, Fla , issue Richard Turnbull, Robert Eugene and Sarah Salina Second wife, Virginia Turnbull, of Monticello, Fla.

Robert Linsey Barry son of Dr Andrew Lawson Barry and Margaret Irvin McDowell, married Laura Augusta Hackett, of Georgia , issue Robert Edwin and Margaret

Robert Edwin Barry married Mary Bryan Thiot, of Savannah, Ga , issue Ruth, Mary Bryan and Robert Andrew. Second marriage, Anna Henderson Green, of Atlanta, Ga ; issue Edwin Joseph

Margaret Bairy married Edwin P Ansley of Atlanta, Ga , issue Laura Barry Ansley and Mamie Ansley

Mary Jane Barry, daughter of Andrew Lawson Barry and Margaret Irvine McDowell, married Dr Adolphus Sherard Fowler, of Georgia issue : Eugene Moore, Minnie Lee, Mary Jane, Hugh Barry and Jessie Euphemia

Eugene Moore married Minnie Riggs, of Forney. Tex , issue Hugh Chilton

Minnie Lee married Melvin Gardner, of Norfolk, Va., issue Dorothy and John Nicklin.

Mary Jane married Roy Nall Cole, of Newnan, Ga

Sarah Ann Barry, daughter of Andrew Lawson Barry and Margaret Irvine McDowell, married William C Sloan, of Georgia, issue . Elizabeth Irvin, Willie Emma, Julia Scott, Thomas Adam, Annie Gertrude, Euphemia, Laura Barry and Robert Andrew

Elizabeth Irvin married Oscar Adam Sloan, of Florida, issue Sarah Eva, Anna May, Andrew Moore and Willie Emma

Willie Emma married Oscar Emerson Ham, of Georgia , issue Alton Sloan, Emma Estelle, Roberthene and Emerson Barry

Julia Scott married Edgar Leslie McDonald, of Georgia, issue   Eddie Claude and Julia Irvin

Thomas Adam married Annie Iola Tye, of Georgia, issue   Thomas Adam, Carl and Wyman

Annie Gertrude married Herbert Greenberry Bryan, of Georgia

Euphemia married William P Bellinger, of Florida

Laura Barry married Joel Echols Smith, Florida

Another descendant of the Irvines of Bonshaw is Rev Dr L W Irvine Porter, of the Radford Presbyterian Church Radford, Va

Rev David C Irwin married Martha Lucretia Pryor, daughter of George E Pryor, M D, of Frederick county, Md., issue   James, Elizabeth, George, Julia, Mary Virginia, William, Leonidas, H David and Lucretia (twins), Mary W and James Emory Irvine (died in infancy)

Elizabeth Willson Irvine, married Pryor Boyd, of Wheeling, W. Va

George Pryor Irvin married Signora J Wilson, daughter of Robert Wilson, of Rockbridge county, Va, issue   Essie L, George Pryor, Elizabeth W (died in infancy)

Julia Sweeney Irvine died in infancy

Mary Virginia Irvine died in infancy.

William Pryor Irwin married Julia Rush Junkin, daughter of Rev. E D Junkin, D. D, issue   Wilfred P, John Preston, Agnes J, Leonidas W (died in infancy), George J

Rev Leonidas Willson Irwin

Lucretia Irwin

Harry David Irwin married Anna White, daughter of Wm S. White, Esq, of Lexington, Va, issue   Frances W

Mary W Irwin

Mrs. Belle Irvine Wharton.

Mrs Belle Irvine Wharton is descended from William Irvine, one of the seven brothers who came from Larne, Ireland, about 1729-30. William Irvine married Anne Craig, who died and was buried in Ireland in the church yard of Raloo, by the side of her daughter Johanna, who had fallen asleep before her

William Irvine and his two sons, David and Christopher, came to America and settled in Bedford county, Va   David Irvine came to Kentucky, and was the progenitor of the Madison county Irvines. Christopher went to Wilkes county, Ga., in 1794

Christopher Irvine married Louisa Tucker, of Amherst, Va, and they had two sons, Charles and Isaiah Tucker   Charles Irvine removed to Richmond, Va, and died there in the early part of the present century   Isaiah Tucker

Irvine, at the age of ten years was taken by his father, Christopher Irvine, to Wilkes county, Ga., in 1794, as before stated

Before leaving Virginia, Christopher Irvine was married the second time, to Miss Echols   They had six sons and one daughter born to them   I have been able to learn the names of but four of these children—Christopher, William, David and Catherine   Mrs Wharton, great-granddaughter of Christopher Irvine, writes· "I think, indeed I know, that Christopher Irvine had, by his marriage with Miss Echols, a son John, and I think he had a son Robert and an Andrew"   These are family names among the Irvines of Bonshaw, from whom Christopher Irvine was descended

Isaiah Tucker Irvine, son of Christopher Irvine and his wife Louisa Tucker, married Isabella Lee Barkston, issue   Louisa, Nancy Herndon, Prudence, Charles Mercia, Mary, Isaiah Tucker, Martha, Lucinda and Stephen. (Stephen died in infancy.)

Charles Mercia Irvine, son of Isaiah Tucker and his wife Isabella Lee Barkston, married Harriette Andrews Battle (sometimes spelled Battaile), had two sons born to him, Reuben and Charles Battle, and one daughter, Mary Isabella, who married Rev Dr M B Wharton, and is the subject of this sketch

The children of Rev. Dr Morton Bryan Wharton and his wife are Charles Irvine (who died in infancy), Harriette Grace and Morton Bryan Harriette Grace Wharton married John McDowell Moore, issue· Wharton Adolphus, Elizabeth Irvine, May Belle, Emma and Bertha Herndon

Morton Bryan Wharton, Jr, married Kitty Holt, issue   one daughter, Mary Catherine

Charles Battle, son of Charles Mercia Irvine and his wife, Harriette Battle, married Mary Speer   His brother, Reuben Battle Irvine, died in infancy   The children of Charles Battle Irvine and his wife, Mary Speer, are two sons, who died in infancy, and three daughters whose names are May Speer, Ruby Lillian and Harriette Battle.   May Speer Irvine, married Logan Crichton, M D ; Charles Barkston Irvine died in infancy, Ruby Lillian Irvine, married Mr Herbert Willis Post

Rev Dr M B. Wharton, husband of Belle Irvine, was born April 5, 1839 He is the son of Malcolm H and Susan R Wharton   He was educated at Richmond College and at the University of Virginia, ordained pastor of the Baptist Church at Bristol, Tenn, in 1862, married Belle Irvine in 1864, elected pastor of the First Baptist Church of Eufaula, Ala, in 1867, and remained there five years, elected pastor of the Walnut Street Baptist Church, Louisville, Ky, in 1872, and remained there three years, elected pastor of the First Baptist Church, Augusta, Ga, in 1876, remaining there one year, elected corresponding secretary of the Southern Baptist Theological Seminary for a time.   In 1881 Dr Wharton was made United States Consul to Germany by President Garfield   After his return to this country from abroad, Dr Wharton became editor of the *Christian Index*, and held that position one year, when he was called to the pastorate of the First Baptist Church of Montgomery, Ala He remained at Montgomery as pastor of the church above mentioned for six years, and in 1897 was called to the Freemason Street Baptist Church of Norfolk, Va., where he now resides

Dr Wharton is a man of wide and varied learning He is a patriot, author, poet and a Christian gentleman whom the South loves to honor He is author of " European Notes, or, What I Saw in the Old World," " Famous Women of the Old Testament," and " Famous Women of the New Testament," and poems many of which will live and move the world long after the hand that penned them is ashes and dust Dr Wharton was made Doctor of Divinity by Washington and Lee University in the year 1876, and the title could have been bestowed on no more worthy follower of the meek and lowly Jesus

He is descended from the younger brother of Sir George Wharton—Lord Thomas Wharton—as follows First Sir George Wharton had sons—George, Thomas, Jesse, John and Joseph , second George had sons—John, Joseph and William , third George had sons—Zachary and Samuel , Samuel Wharton had sons—William, John, Joseph, Samuel and Malcom , Malcom Wharton had sons—William, Joseph, John, Samuel, Morton Bryan, Malcom Frederick and Henry Marion   Morton Bryan Wharton married Belle Irvine, and has a son, Morton Bryan Wharton, who married Kitty Holt

The arms of the Whartons (as borne by Philip Wharton, the celebrated Duke of Wharton,) are. Sa a maunch ar within a bordure or, charged with eight pairs of lion's paws saltireways, erased gu , the bordure being an augmentation granted by Edward VI   Crest, a Moor, kneeling, in coat of mail, all ppr. ducally crowned or, stabbing himself with a sword of the first, hilt and pommel of the second. Another crest, and the one used by Rev. Dr M B Wharton, is: A bull's head erased ar., attired or, gorged with a ducal coronet, per pale of the second and gu. The arms of the Irvines of Bonshaw (Irish branch), from whom his wife is descended, are thus described Ar a fesse gu betw three holly leaves, ppr. Crest, a dexter arm in armor, fesseways, issuant out of a cloud, hand ppr holding a thistle, also ppr motto, " *Dum memor ipse mei* "

Mrs. Martha Irvine Battle, daughter of Isaiah Tucker Irvine was described by Richard Malcolm Johnson as "a girl that was simply glorious " In a recent letter from Baltimore to a kinsman of Mrs Battle, he says. " I should rather see Mat Battle than any one now alive " How I should like to see a woman who receives praise from such a man as Georgia's most gifted son, whose pen pictures are like the paintings of Hogarth, easy to understand, but never to be imitated or surpassed in this world.

Hon. Wilbur F. Browder, of Russellville, Ky.

Wilbur F Browder is descended from the Irvines of Bonshaw, in the following line Alexander Irvine, married Sophia Gault, issue Andrew, William and Christopher, born in the North of Ireland Alexander, his wife and sons came to Bedford county, Va Alexander Irvine and his wife died the same day William Irvine, brother of Alexander, reared Andrew Irvine, who was eight years old at the time of his father's death. The Irvines of Pennsylvania reared Christopher and William, and I have never been able to rely upon any information that has been given me concerning them Some say that William was a General in the Revolution, but I have never been able to prove it to my satisfaction There was one William Irvine, a General in the Revolution, but, if he was Andrew's brother, it has not been made plain to me

Andrew Irvine, married Elizabeth Mitchell, daughter of Elizabeth Innes and William Mitchell, of Edinburgh, Scotland Caleb Irvine, son of Elizabeth Mitchell and Andrew Irvine, married Elizabeth Ewing Mitchell; issue Norval, Thomas, Caleb Ewing, Robert Green and Elizabeth Eleanor Elizabeth Eleanor Irvine, married Rev David Browder, November 18, 1842, issue: Bettie Green, James Thomas, Robert Irvine, Wilbur Fisk, born December 12, 1848, Helen Mary, David, Caleb Ewing, Richard, Edward McClure and Fannie Irvine The children of David Browder and his wife, are all dead except three sons, Hon Wilbur F Browder, of Russellville, Ky , and Edward McClure, now living in Arizona, and Richard, now living with his wife and five children, in Montgomery, Ala

Wilbur F Browder was graduated from the University of Virginia in 1868, and from the Law Department of the Kentucky University in November, 1869, and has since that time been distinguished in his profession in this and other states

On January 18, 1872, Mr Browder married Bettie Bernard Wills, a great-niece of Geo M Bibb The children of this marriage are Wilbur Fisk, Marion Castner, John Caleb, Lucien McClure and Eugene Irvine

Wilbur Fisk Browder, born November 23, 1872, married Hattie Martin Frayer, November 23, 1893, and has a son, Wilbur Fisk Browder (third), born February 19, 1895

Marion Castner Browder, graduated from Bethel College, June, 1892, and from University of Virginia, June, 1894, and from University of Berlin, Germany, in 1895

John Caleb Browder is now a student at the University of Virginia

Lucy McClure Browder is a student at Bethel College, and the youngest son, Eugene Irvine Browder, is at a private school at Russellville, Ky

Caleb Irvine, son of Andrew and Elizabeth Irvine, was drowned in Mayfield creek in 1835 He w an e s the summer but in attempting to cross

Mayfield creek, swollen by recent rains, his horse threw him. He must have been hurt in the fall, for he never came to the surface of the stream. His wife walked the shore of the stream, day and night, until the water subsided and her husband's body was found. He was clinging to the roots of a tree that overhung the water. His wife lived until 1868, and died at the house of her son-in-law, Mr. Browder, in Montgomery, Ala., at the advanced age of eighty-five years.

Caleb Ewing Irvine, son of Caleb above mentioned, was born a few weeks after his father's death. He was educated at West Point and became Lieutenant in the United States Army and served with great distinction in the war with Mexico. After the war was over he was ordered to the far West to quell an outbreak of a certain turbulent tribe of Indians. In the fight with these savages he was, in some way, cut off from his command, and his soldiers, fearing the worst, after the skirmish was over crept back to learn his fate. Lieutenant Irvine's command was outnumbered, ten to one, by the Indians. They saw Irvine bound to a stake and faggots piled around him. Not being able to rescue their commander, and determined not to witness his suffering, they fled. When they had rallied a sufficient number of troops to attempt his rescue they returned to the spot where they had seen him tied to the stake. There had been a fire but no charred remains of a body could be found. Nevertheless, Lieutenant Irvine was reported dead.

How he escaped being burned by the Indians, my informant did not know, but some time after Lieutenant Irvine resigned his commission in the army. If his resignation was published his relatives did not see it, and they mourned him as dead for many years. He went to the wilds of Oregon and made himself a home, and his existence was not known to his relatives and friends until 1885, when he was discovered by his great-nephew, Judge Robert Green Irvine, son of Lieutenant Irvine's nephew of the same name. Judge Robert Green Irvine was Circuit Judge of Butte City Judicial District and Montana Territory, and was, for many years, a very influential and popular Democrat of that part of the country.

Why Lieutenant Irvine acted in this manner toward his relatives and friends he never made known to any one. He was one of the most handsome and soldierly-looking men of his time, and his record in the army, whether in active service or in camp, was without blemish.

Judge Robert Green Irvine died in 1892 at Deer Lodge, Montana.

Rev. Robert Green Irvine, son of Caleb Irvine and Elizabeth Ewing Mitchell, his wife, was a minister of great eloquence and prominence in the M. E. Church, South, and died at Columbia, Tenn., in 1892, beloved and mourned by a host of friends.

Robert Ewing Irvine is unmarried and lives in the old Irvine homestead at Columbia, Tenn.

The McElroys.

The arms of the McElroys, from whom the McElroys of this country are descended, are described as follows Or on a bend azure, a star of six points between two crescents argent, and in base a bow and arrow of the second Crest — A hand, erect, holding a battle axe ppr   Motto — Trusty and true

I subjoin a letter from a friend in Ireland, Mary Semple, and make no apology for copying it word for word

MOUNTHILL, LARNE. IRELAND, October 12, 1897.

My Dear Mrs Boyd   * * * The McElroys, some of them, live about a mile from here   The first of the name who came here was Charles McElroy He was a soldier, stationed at Carrickfergus Castle, and came in the army of Gen Robert Monroe, who was sent here in the wars of 1641   That was a fearful time.   There was a great battle fought near Larne on a hill that was called Shinei-roe, where General Monroe was slain, and the hill takes its name (in part) from General Monroe

This McElroy distinguished himself at that battle, as did many others McElroy was of the party who chased Phelim Roe O'Neill, of Shane's Castle, near Antrim Town, off the battlefield.   He was rewarded for his gallant services with some fine land near Ballyclare, where some of his descendants now reside Others of his descendants live at Ballymena.

Charles McElroy was a native of Inverness Shire, Scotland, and the fierce highland blood that ran in his veins fires some of his descendants to this day I knew one of them, one William McElroy, and like his ancestor, Charles, he was an old soldier and had five medals   He was the first man to place his foot on the heights of Alma

✦   ❋   ✳   ╚   ✳   ✛

The churchyard of Raloo covers about a half acre of ground   The walls of an old church are still standing, although the church was burned by the Catholics in 1641   In this old church were all the records of the Scottish families who had settled here   They were all destroyed by the fire that burned the church   But every family handed down its own records and arms   The arms are contained in an old book, hundreds of years old   If a neighbor knew the ancestry of one who was not versed in his own lineage, he gave it to him, that it might be preserved.

The dear old churchyard of Raloo holds the dust of many of your ancestors—the Fords, Gaults, and at the eastern corner, on which the first beams of the rising sun rest, sleep the Irvines, among them kinsmen, the Wylies

I do not think you quite understood what I wrote you concerning Alexander Irvine, who killed the man in Scotland, on the hunting field   He was a brother to Robert, who was the founder of the Irvine family here, in the early part of

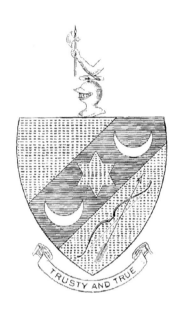

TRUSTY AND TRUE

the sixteenth century, and great-uncle to Alexander (one of the seven brothers
who came to America in 1729-30), from whom you are descended. Alexan
der, your immediate ancestor, was the son of James Irvine and Sophia Gault,
his wife, and Alexander married his kinswoman, a Miss Gault

Affectionately yours,

MARY SEMPLE.

I think the mistake is made by Miss Semple, as I have stated before. The
tradition has been handed down in my mother's family, from generation to
generation

The following pages were sent to me by Mr William T Knott, of Lebanon, Ky

I send you the following notes from my manuscript sketches of the McElroy's,
of Kentucky, who married with the Irvine family. The McElroys are a
numerous family, widely distributed throughout the United States, from the
Atlantic to the Pacific and from the Lakes to the Gulf. First immigration—the
original families were from North Ireland, County Down, and adjacent localities,
were not only all Protestants, but Presbyterians of no uncertain type. Some
of them were members of the Old Covenanters and some of the Associate
Church or Seceders

About the year 1730, James McElroy, with his young bride, Sarah
McHugh (or McCune), sailed on the vessel "George and Anne," in company
with the Irvines, McDowells, McCunes (or McHughs) and others. They first
settled, on the borders of Pennsylvania, in New Jersey or Delaware, thence
farther west in Pennsylvania, and later the families of James McElroy and
John Irvine, a Presbyterian minister, moved South and settled in Campbell
county, Va. James McElroy had five sons. John, Archibald, Hugh,
Samuel and James. John and Archy were married (the names of their wives
not known) and moved to South Carolina. Their descendants are scattered
over the Southern States from the Carolinas to Texas. The third, fourth and
fifth sons, Hugh, Samuel and James, married three sisters, Esther, Mary and
Margaret Irvine, daughters of John Irvine, mentioned above. John Irvine's
children were John, Esther, Nancy, Mary, Elizabeth and Margaret. While
in Pennsylvania during the French and Indian Wars, Nancy was captured by
the Indians and held prisoner for a few days, when she was rescued by her
friends

In the year 1786 or '87, Hugh McElroy and his brother-in-law, John
Irvine, moved from Campbell county, Va., to Kentucky, Irvine settling
near where is now the city of Danville, Boyle county, Hugh McElroy settled
near where is now Springfield, Washington county

In the autumn of 1789, Samuel and James McElroy followed, Samuel
settling about four miles east, and James one mile south-west, of where is now
the city of Lebanon, Ma   Hugh McElroy and Father Irvine, his

5

wife, had ten children, six sons and four daughters   Samuel McElroy and
Mary Irvine, his wife, had thirteen children, eight sons and five daughters
James McElroy and Margaret Irvine, his wife, had eleven children, three sons
and eight daughters

The descendants of the three McElroy boys and their Irvine wives, may
be found in almost every State of the Union

The children of Hugh McElroy and Esther Irvin were as follows
1   James, married Rosa Hardin and (second) a widow, Mrs Pickett
2   Margaret, married William Muldraugh, whose father gave his name to
     Muldraugh Hill
3   Sarah, married ———— Sandusky, a son of an old pioneer
4   Mary, married John Simpson (first) and John McElroy (second hus-
     band)
5   John, married Miss Hundley, his descendants are the Springfield
     McElroys
6   Hugh, married Miss Dorsey, some of his descendants lived in Hardin
     county, Ky
7   Samuel, married Mary Wilson, many of his descendants moved to
     Missouri
8   Robert, married Miss Hundley, his descendants live in Washington
     and Marion counties, Ky
9   William, married Miss Crawford, and left two children, lived in Marion
     county, Ky
10 Elizabeth, never married, lived to a good old age, in Springfield, Ky

The children of Samuel McElroy and Mary Irvin were as follows
1   Sarah, born 1767, married Alexander Handley, their descendants live
     in southern Kentucky
2   John, born 1769, married Miss Copeland (first) and Mrs Mary Simp-
     son, his cousin (second wife)
3   James, born 1770, died young.
4   Hugh, born 1772, married Miss Gilkie, had only one son, Hiram, a
     noted lawyer in his day   The McElroys of Union county, Ky, are
     his descendants
5   Margaret, born 1773, married James Wilson, their descendants live in
     Mississippi and Arkansas
6   Abram, born 1774, died young
7. William, born 1776, married twice—first, Miss Keturah Cleland, sister
     to Rev Dr Thomas Cleland, of Providence Church, Mercer county,
     second wife was Miss Mary Kirk. Ex-Governor J Proctor Knott is
     his grandson by his first wife, Miss Cleland
8   Samuel, born in 1777, married twice   First wife, Miss Minnie Briggs,
     second wife, Miss Lum H. Grundy

9. Mary, born in 1778, married William McColgan, had no children
10 James, born in 1780, married Esther Simpson, moved to Missouri
11 Abram, born in 1780, married Miss Radford, moved to Christian
    county, Ky (James and Abram were twins)
12 Elizabeth, born in 1782, married George Wilson, and moved to
    Indiana
13 Nancy, born in 1785, married Mr Robbins, moved to Indiana

The children of James McElroy and Margaret Irvine were as follows
1 John, died in young manhood, not married
2. Sarah, died young
3 Elizabeth, married General Allen
4 Margaret, married Dr. Blythe
5 Mary, married (first) Allen, and (second) Speed
6 Sarah, died young
7. Nancy, died young.
8 Esther, married Felix B Grundy.
9 James A , married Mary Irvine, and moved to Missouri
10 William I , married Jane Muldrow, and moved to Missouri

The ancestors of this trio of McElroy boys who married the three Irvine
girls were originally from Scotland   Tradition says that during the religious
persecution in Scotland three brothers, McElroys, went from Argyle and Lan-
ark counties, Scotland, one from each county, and one from Glasgow, and
settled in County Down, Ireland, purchasing large landed estates and from
those three brothers, the McElroys in North Ireland and immigrants to America
had their origin

James Callaway.

James Callaway, the subject of this sketch, is descended from William
Irvine, one of the seven brothers who came to America between 1721 and
1730

William Irvine married Ann Craig, who was of noble blood, in Ireland
Three children were born to them—Johanna, Christopher and David   William
Irvine's wife died and was buried in the churchyard of Raloo near Mounthill,
Larne, Ireland, beside her daughter, Johannah, who had died a short time
before   William and his two sons, Christopher and David, came to America
They landed at Philadelphia, Pa , and afterwards removed to Bedford county,
Va   David Irvine came to Kentucky, and Christopher Irvine went to Wilkes
county, Ga   I quote from a letter written by James Callaway, for a Southern
periodical   ''Christopher Irvine settled the old Irvine plantation, in 1796.   It
is yet in the Irvine family owned by Luther Cason, whose wife is a lineal

descendant, a great-granddaughter of Christopher's son, Isaiah Tucker Irvine. Christopher Irvine's wife was Louisa Tucker, of Virginia This Christopher Irvine, a far-off descendant of Christopher Irvine, who commanded the light horse for King James IV. at the battle of Flodden Hill, or, as Sir Walter Scott, in "Marmion," has it, "Flodden Field," was a captain of a Virginia company in the Revolutionary War, and, for service in the army, impressed a yoke of steers belonging to John Hook, a Tory, for which Hook sued him after the war He was defended by Patrick Henry Old-time schoolboys, like Bill Arp, Robert J Bacon or Richard Malcolm Johnston remember Henry's speech In impassioned rhetoric he presented the hardships of the war, the great struggle for independence, pictured the general rejoicing of the people, and while all America was shouting for joy, for victory won, here comes one Hook, crying "Beef, beef!"

Christopher, son of William Irvine and Annie Craig, married Louisa Tucker Issue Charles and Isaiah Tucker

Isaiah Tucker Irvin married Isabella Lee Barkston Issue Charles Mercia, Isaiah Tucker, Stephen (who died in infancy), Nancy Henderson, Prudence, Caroline Carter, Mary Anne, Martha and Louisa

Mary Anne Irvine, married first, John Walton Issue Belle, who married Robert Bacon (and who reared A O Bacon, U S Senator from Georgia), John and Stokes After the death of John Walton, Mary Anne Irvine married Merrel Price Callaway Issue Merrel, Henry Irvine, James and Isaiah Tucker.

James Callaway married the accomplished and beautiful Vieva Flewellyn Furlow, daughter of Col. T M Furlow and Margaret Holt. Margaret Holt was the daughter of Tarplay Holt, son of Simon Holt, who had eight sons and one daughter This only daughter married a Mr Colquitt, and was the mother of the celebrated Walter T Colquitt, and grandmother of General Alfred H. Colquitt

The children of James Callaway and his wife, Vieva F Furlow, are Merrel, James Woodpin, Margaret Holt, Mary Irvin, Henry Irvin, Kate and Holt

Mr. Callaway was a Confederate soldier He responded to the call of his country at the early age of sixteen, and was quartermaster and commissary sergeant of his regiment, the Third Georgia Reserves In South Carolina, where his regiment held Fort Coosawhatchee, the exposure to shot and shell was great Mr Callaway's duties required him to daily cross the bridge over the Tulafinee river and the long trestle across the swamp in shooting distance of the Federal sharpshooters A solitary plank ran across this trestle and bridge, and each trip was fraught with danger Though running the gauntlet of shot and shell and whizzing bullets safely, he was not proof against swamp miasma, and for weeks he lay prostrate with typho-malarial fever Medicines there were none—not even a lemon, and nothing but pluck and the hope of meeting his mother again inspired strength to pull through the terrible ordeal.

Mr Callaway graduated from Mercer University in 1868 After marriage he lived the quiet life of a farmer in Mitchell county, Georgia His wife's health required a change, and in 1885 he became editor of the Albany "News and Advertiser " In the fall of 1886 he took work with the Macon "Telegraph," and is yet a member of its staff. As a writer he is easy and graceful and his contributions to his paper are perused with pleasure by its readers

Mr Callaway's mother was a glorious type of the old Southern matron She had intellect enough to rule an empire and love enough to save the world Her father was Isaiah Tucker Irvin, a man whose very appearance bespoke the nobleman He was a king among men, yet so thoroughly democratic in nature and manners that the humblest approached him with ease and confidence Indeed, his grand old home was Liberty Hall to all comers.

Writing of his grandfather, Mr Callaway says " My grandfather was not so tall of stature, but his magnificent presence produced the impression of Louis XIV, whom people thought over six feet, but who in reality was only five feet eight inches He amassed a large fortune and entertained royally His beverage was " cherry bounce," and it put to shame any mint julep brewed by the Virginians. His home was twelve miles from Washington, Ga Before reaching his house you ascended a hill, on the brow of which were large and venerable chestnut trees, with wide-spreading shades, in front of which was his country store, from which a broad driveway led to the hospitable home. Near by was the spring and that celebrated spring-house where melons and apple cider and ' good things ' were stored More remarkable was Mrs Irvin, a granddaughter of Joseph Henderson Of Mrs Irvin General Robert Toombs was especially fond, and while hiding out from the Federal soldiery after the war, he sought on a dark night Mrs Irvin's room in Washington, Ga , and spent hours in conversing with her about his own father and mother and ' old times ' in Wilkes county

"It seems to my childish recollections, ' continues Mr Callaway, "that my grandfather s blacksmith shop was a half a mile from the house, but it must not have been, for grandfather, when he wished to give orders to 'Sol, the blacksmith, would step to the edge of his porch and call out, 'S-o-l, you, S-o-l-o-m-o-n!' and the response always came 'S-i-r!'"

In starting life, Isaiah Tucker Irvin was sometimes in need of money, His neighbor, Beasley, was rich, dressed in purple and fine linen, wore a hat that told of pride of purse, on his hands were big gloves, and he drove fine horses One day Major Irvin approached Beasley seated in his buggy and requested a loan of $100 Beasley treated him rather haughtily and drove on, but not before Major Irvin could say to him· " Beasley, I'll have my revenge " Beasley, the fast young man, by high living and fast driving, and careless habits came to want, and all his houses and lands and negroes and mules and horses were put up for sale Everything was knocked down to I T Irvin Irvin bought all Beasley possessed The sale over, Beasley approached Major Irvin and said "Major, you· hod you revenge allow me to redeem my family pictures " Major Irvin turned to Beasley and said " Yes, be a man, Beasley, and redeem all, and Beasley turned over a new leaf He became a man and redeemed his property

This story illustrates the man, Isaiah T Irvin He hurt no man when down, but extended the hand of generosity His grandchildren love his very name, which hangs, like a memory keepsake, around the neck of each of them

Isaiah Tucker Irvin, son of Isaiah T Irvin and Isabella Henderson Bankston, was born May 25, 1819, in Wilkes county, Ga He was aboard the steamer Bayou City, plying between Galveston and Houston, along with O L Battle and M P Callaway, his brothers-in-law, going to his farm in Texas, when the steamer exploded her boiler on the night of September 27, 1860 He was seen rushing aft, and it was thought he fell overboard

Mr Irvin was a graduate of the State University at Athens and divided the first honors with Professor S P Sanford, who became the distinguished professor of mathematics of Mercer University Mr Irvin chose the law as his life profession, in which he became distinguished He ranked with the first statesmen of Georgia

His friend and neighbor, Gen Robt Toombs, then United States senator from Georgia, was at Hancock Superior Court when came to him the news of Irvin's death This distinguished Senator, in subdued and saddened tone, remarked " In Washington (Ga), to-day, every man, woman and child, white and black, will be in mourning and in tears, and more than all, their sorrow is sincere He was the friend of everyone, and everyone was his friend "

At the time of his death I. T. Irvin was speaker of the Georgia House of Representatives, and the Committee on Resolutions, reporting, say " Resolved, That in his death the state has sustained incalculable loss in her public councils, this House has been deprived of a presiding officer rarely equaled and never surpassed in efficiency, fairness and courtesy, society has lost one of its most useful members, and the cause of morality and religion a faithful defender "

Mr Irvin had served for years also in the Georgia Senate, and Gen. A R Lawton, of Chatham, said· " I T Irvin was a true son of Georgia All his heart and talents were devoted to her interests and prosperity * ~ < It is a sad thing, Mr. President, to lose him in this hour of Georgia s peril It is a sad thing that heaven can not spare those whom earth so much needs "

Mr Turner, of Putnam, among other things so eulogistic of Speaker Irvin, said· " The highest honors of the land were clustering around his head, and the graces scarcely crowned his temples with one wreath ere the hand of patriotic friendship twined another for his blushing brow The people of Georgia desired to have his hand at the helm We wanted for our state executive Isaiah Tucker Irvin We wanted our friend, but God wanted him too, and He said to His servant, Come up higher "

Mr. McGee, of Houston, addressing the Assembly, said " And what an example, sir, did he furnish for his countrymen, his children and his surviving associates of this legislature An example so worthy of their admiration and of their imitation, and one illustrating so beautifully the object of his creation."

These expressions from his comrades of the legislature are not flattery Isaiah T Irvin was an ideal man—the ideal statesman He was never false to his faith, a man who was never false to his honor, a statesman who was never false to his country. His home life was beautiful, and his children revere his memory, and in Wilkes county to-day, after all the hardships of war, and the trials and humiliations since the war, Irvin's name is a synonym for all that is pure in character, and noble and lofty in manhood

> "Sweet Hope, of all consolers best art thou!
> Thy soothing balm has staunched the bloody flow
> A stream of blissful peace flows through our souls,
> For him whose loss we mourned hast thou restored,
> And with him given the rapturous joys of heaven '

The Drummer's Life.

The Ups and Downs of the Man on the Road

To the uninitiated a poetic charm rests about the life of a drummer By such he is regarded as a sort of commercial butterfly, flying here and there, sipping the sweets from that which most attracts him Indeed, Charles Dickens, the closest of observers, falls somewhat into this error himself, for in describing the uncommercial traveler, he allows the said uncommercial traveler to thus introduce himself "No landlord is my friend and brother, no chamber-maid loves me no waiter worships me, no boots admires and envies me, no round of beef or tongue or ham is expressly cooked for me, no label advertisement is personally addressed to me no hotel room, tapestried with great coats and railway wrappers, is set apart for me, no house of public entertainment in the United Kingdom greatly cares for my opinion of its brandy or sherry '

But the man of whom I speak—the commercial traveler, the drummer, the soliciting agent—does not rest on a bed of flowers His life is a prosaic one His is a life of toil and work Success does not fall upon him as the dews from heaven, but he has to work out his own salvation His victories are sweat victories and labor victories, won by hard daily toil

Sometimes his lines are cast in pleasant places, and the "nomadic" salesman seems to enjoy life, but if a "tramp," he is not of that species that sits down to rest by the wayside the tramp offensive is always hunting work but

never finds it, the drummer is forever "on the go" and always at work There
is nothing pastoral or meditative about the drummer, he belongs to the positive,
or indicative, not the subjunctive mood, his work does not permit him to loiter
or idle, as does the unharnessed horse when listlessly feeding in his pasture

Macon owes much to her traveling men They are her representatives,
her upbuilders, her developers, her banner-bearers. Like diplomats in foreign
countries, who seek to uphold the honor and majesty of the mother country
and advance her glory, these selfsame traveling representatives embody in themselves Macon's sentiment and spirit and enterprise, and at all times, in season
and out of season, they labor for her growth and prosperity

To accomplish this is no small work They have to bring to their aid all
the genius, the energy, the intelligence, the pluck, the eloquence, the patience,
the forbearance they can command They are indeed heroes in the strife, and
heroes worthy of all honors Were soldiers ever more valiant than Bill Pope,
S E Harris, Ben McNeice, Levi Anderson, H Wood, Albert Hillsman, Henry
Hatch, Bob Smith, Andrew Kennedy, Lee Happ, Joe Polhill, Lee Ellis, Jake
Emanuel, Ed Isaacs, Jim Bateman, Lee Watson, Tom Trammell, John Walden
and others who fight Macon's battles night and day—resting not, ceasing not,
till their efforts are crowned with victory?

Nor is the drummer's life all sunshine He meets difficulties. He en-
counters storms With ardent hopes he approaches yon merchant Does he
get a sympathetic greeting? Not every time Some merchants, at the very
presence of the drummer, bristle up like a fretted porcupine and pelt the
fellow with quills of obnoxious frowns and ill-nature until there is nothing to
do but retreat—the drummer always retreats in a masterly manner

But storms come in other ways Winds blow, rains descend, the drummer must "get there all the same" His business is to get there. He must
sell. That's what he is hired for No storms nor rain nor porcupines must prevent If so, then the drummer becomes "the back number"—not the "man
you are hunting for' The employer looks for the "returns" The results
must appear, else he steps down and out His only safety is in success. Honor
and shame, they tell us, from no condition rise, act well your part and there
the honor lies. The drummer has to act well—i e, he has to succeed Ex-
cuses are not in order And what it costs in toil, labor, push and mental tra-
vail and effort, traveling by night and working by day, to achieve success! A
hero, indeed, is the successful drummer

But this selfsame drummer is a jolly, good fellow You enjoy meeting him
He is a hearty handshaker He is cheery, blithe as a bird of song, and throws
off care with the abandon of a child He has to be, the law of success puts this
demand upon him If his heart is troubled, that face of his must be wreathed
in smiles The drummer, too, is high-toned, generous, and his frailties lean to
virtue's side He is not a dude, and affects not silk and velvet, but he discards
shabby clothes as impediments to success. The "blues" he must not have

Call in "the boys of the road" and give them Christmas cheer Extend the wassail bowl and let them dance and sing, for "Christmas comes but once a year '   JAMES CALLAWAY

The Adams Branch of the Irvine Family, of Bedford County, Va.

Compiled by Miss Juliet Fauntleroy, of Lynch's Station, Va, and Mrs. George Boykin Saunders, of Atlanta, Ga., with the Assistance of W. G. Stannard, of Richmond , Robert W Carroll, of Cincinnati, and other Noted Genealogists, etc.

James Adams, the third son of Captain Robert Adams, Jr of the Revolution, and his wife, Penelope Lynch, married Mary Irvine, daughter of David Irvine, and his wife, Jane Kyle, of Bedford county, Va , and granddaughter of William Irvine These Irvines were of Scottish descent, and descended from Robert Bruce The crest most used by the American Irvines is a knight's helmet surmounted by a holly branch, with the motto "Sub sole sub umbra virens " Mrs Sophia Fox Sea, of Louisville, Ky , has this to say about the Irvines " There were sixteen Irvine coats of arms, eleven of which have the holly branch or leaves What a family it must have been in point of standing They are descended from Robert Bruce, the first Irvine, William de Irvine, having married a granddaughter of Bruce, and daughter of Lord Douglas, and from whom branched the 'great Irvine families' spoken of in history. Read the ' Abbot ' again and see what Walter Scott has to say of the holly branch, the ancient insignia of the house," etc

James Adams and Mary Irvine were married May 4, 1776, and their marriage license is recorded at Bedford county court house, Va The Adams family were old settlers of Virginia, having located first near Williamsburg and later on, some of them settling in what is now Campbell and Bedford counties The first American ancestor of the Adamses, came from the Island of Anglesea, North Wales, and it is a mooted question whether he came directly to the old "James River Settlement" in Virginia, or settled in one of the New England states, and thence his posterity drifted to the "Old Dominion " The name of the "emigrant ancestor" is said to have been William Adams, but on this point there is no certainty Robert Adams, Sr (father of Captain Robert or "Robin" Adams, Jr., of the Revolution), was the grandson of one "Robert Addams," who, about the year 1620, was a member of the first "House of Burgesses" in Virginia Robert Adams, Sr , married Mary, the daughter of William Lewis For mention of the Robert Adams of 1620, see Hening's "Statutes at Large of Virginia " Robert Adams, Jr., and his wife, Penelope Lynch, had two sons who fought in the Revolution. These sons were Robert Adams, who married Mary Terrill the daughter of Joel Terrill and Anna

Lewis, and James Adams who married Mary Irvine In the "land office" at
the Capitol in Richmond, it is recorded that James Adams ranked as "cor-
poral" in the Revolutionary army, and was granted land bounty for services in
said army. There is also, in the same office a record of bounty lands being
granted to "Robert Adams, a soldier in the Revolutionary army," and this
Robert Adams, as we know, was the father of James Adams The following
extracts from a letter written by Mr Robert W Carroll, to Mrs. Saunders,
will be of interest

    "We people who study genealogies are a kind of guild, and are bound by
all the laws of courtesy and comradeship to help one another in emergencies,
etc I write this in business shape, so that if I am able to tell you any facts
you wish to preserve you will have them in form for filing

    "To take your questions seriatim First, you mention a genealogy of the
Adams family How far back does that go in the Virginia line? My information goes thus far Robert Adams, who went into the Revolution with Captain, afterwards Colonel, Harry Terrill, a son of Joel Terrill, Sr., married Mary
Terrill, a daughter of Joel Terrill, Jr , and of Anna Lewis (this Anna Lewis
being a daughter of David Lewis and Anna Terrill), Joel, Jr. and Anna being
first cousins This Robert Adams, was a son of Robert Adams, Jr (known
popularly as 'Captain Bob'), who married Penelope Lynch, sister of Colonel
Charles Lynch and daughter of Charles Lynch and Sarah Clark Robert Adams,
Jr , of the Revolution, must have been at the time of the war, in his prime,
say, from forty-five to fifty years of age, and as he was called Junior, his father,
Robert Adams, must have been living during the Revolution This Captain
Robert Adams, Jr , was one of the first justices of the county court of Campbell county, at its organization in February, 1782 Robert Adams, Jr , was
a son of Robert Adams and Mary Lewis, and was probably born anywhere
from 1718 to 1725, or possibly later His sister, Judith Adams, was born in
1716, and married Micajah Clark, a son of Christopher Clark (Micajah having
been born in 1718—junior of his wife) I think they were married about 1737

    "I can not go back of this Robert Adams, but he must have been born in
the Seventeenth Century—say from 1690 to 1700, possibly earlier. He had a
daughter born in 1716—was probably married a year or more before, and was
most likely twenty years of age, more or less, at the time This guessing calculation takes him back to 1695, or thereabout The name 'Robert' seems
to have been so regularly used, that we may fairly assume that it had been
handed down I find from Hening's 'Statutes of Virginia,' that one Robert
Addams was a member of the first House of Burgesses in Virginia, about 1620
My guess is, that this Robert Adams, was the founder of the Adams family,
of Virginia

                 ⁂   ⁂   ⁂   ⁑

    "Before dropping the Adamses I may add, that Mrs M. A. (Mary Adams,
I suppose) Maverick, of San Antonio, Texas, is a granddaughter of Robert

Adams and Mary Terrill and so on back. She had the tradition that she was a Lynch, but did not have the line. She spoke of it to my cousin, Mrs Elizabeth Williams Perry, of this city, who mentioned it to me, and I was able to trace it up, though at first I was confused by the existence of two Robert Adamses, who were Revolutionary soldiers. Mrs Maverick's daughter married E. H. Terrill, of the line of Henry Terrill (first) who was our Minister to Belgium under Harrison. So that the Terrell and Adams and Lynch bloods were again commingled. Second. As to Governor Charles Lynch and his descendants if he had any, I know but little that is accurate. There were four Charles Lynches. The immigrant (died 1753) Colonel Charles, of the Revolution (died in 1796), Colonel Charles again, who removed to Kentucky, and was probably born about 1756 or '57—his parents having been married January 10th or 12th, 1755. I found that he was figuring about 1803 in the Burr movement to the Southwest—not as a follower of Burr, but as a seller of land to him. At Burr's trial for treason, he testified that he had sold Burr some three hundred and fifty thousand acres of land on the Wichita river, in what is now Arkansas, which Burr said he wanted to colonize. His son Charles, if the eldest, was probably born, say, about 1780, so that when he became Governor of Mississippi, in 1838, he was, say, fifty-eight years of age. He lived some twenty years longer. Third. As to the Terrell in Texas, who is minister to Turkey, I have a "dead sure thing" on his descent. His father was a doctor, but I am not certain of the name, whilst I think it was Christopher. His grandfather was Edward Terrell, whose wife was a Johnson. His great-grandfather was David Terrell (second), who married three scions of the Johnson family during his checkered matrimonial career. This David was the eldest son of David (first) and a brother of Micajah Terrell, my ancestor, who married Sarah Lynch, daughter of the 'immigrant'. David (first) was brother of Henry (first), of Joel, Sr, of Anna Lewis, and of several others, and they were the children of William and Susanna Terrell, beyond whom we have not been able to go with any certainty. Anne Terrell, daughter of Henry (first), married Colonel Charles Lynch, January 10 or 12, 1755, in Quaker meeting, she being about fourteen or fifteen years of age. On the same day her sister Betty, two years older, married Zachariah Moorman, whose mother, Rachel, was a daughter of old Christopher Clark. I had A. W. Terrell's genealogy, back to Henry (second), from himself, etc. He has a silver mounted jug, which tradition says, was brought from England some two hundred years ago, by our ancestress, Anne Terrell. Fourth, as to the other Texas Terrells, Robert Adams Terrell, born at Murfreesboro, Tenn., was a son of James Terrell, of Virginia. He was born in 1820, his parents moved to Boone county, Ky, in 1830, and thence to Booneville, Mo, in 1835. He afterwards went to Kaufman county, Texas His mother had a brother, 'Kit' (Christopher) Adams, at Iberville Parish, La. Terrell, Texas, was named after him. He had a brother, George Whitfield. They all seem to have been prominent in Texas. John I. Terrell, an

attorney at Terrell, Texas, is a son of R. A (Robert Adams) Terrell   I have
no doubt these were the Terrells you were thinking of," etc   [End of extract
from Mr Carroll's letter of April 5, 1896]

The Adams family have always claimed a high descent, tracing back from
Charles the Bald, of France, to Charlemagne, through their ancestress, Princess
Gundred, a daughter of William the Conqueror, who married William de
Warren, the Earl of Surrey, who died in 1089, leaving, among other children,
one Lady Editha de Warren, who married Gerald de Gournai, and had a son,
Hugh de Gournai, who married first, Beatrix, daughter of the Count of
Vermandois, on her death he married Millicent, daughter of Lord Courcy,
and they had a son, Hugh de Gournai, who died in 1180, having married Lady
Julia Damp-Martin, and by this marriage there were two children, Ansaline
and Boison de Gournai   Borson married and had a son, Robert, who married
and was father of John de Gournai, and this John married a lady named
"Olivia," and had but one child, Lady Elizabeth de Gournai or Gourney, who
married Sir John Ap Adam, of Wales, in 1291   Sir John Ap Adam died in
1309, and it is from him and his wife Elizabeth that the American Adamses
descended

For mention of the marriage of Princess Gundred and the Earl of Surrey,
see preface to Doyle's "Official Baronage of England," under the head of
"marriages "   "The History of the Adams Family," by Henry Whittemore,
and published by Willis McDonald & Co, of New York City, has this to say
of the English Adamses

" The earliest record of the English branch of the Adams family, is that
of John Ap Adam, of Charlton Adam, in Somersetshire, who married Elizabeth,
daughter of and heiress to John, Lord Gourney, of Beviston and Tidenham,
county of Gloucestershire, who was summoned to Parliament as Baron of the
Realm, 1296 to 1307   In the upper part of a gothic window on the southeast
side of Tidenham church, near Chopston, the name of 'Johes AB Adam,
1310,' and 'Arms Argent, on a cross gules, five mullets, or,' of Lord Ap
Adam, are still to be found beautifully executed in stained glass of great thick-
ness and in perfect preservation   It originally stood within the boundary of
Wales, but at a later period the boundary line was changed and it now stands
on English soil   The arms and crest borne by the family are described as—
Arms Argent, on a cross gules, five mullets, or   Crest Out of a ducal coronet, a demi-lion   Motto 'Loyal au Mort.'   A motto commonly used by
this branch of the Adams family (the Northern branch) is 'Aspire, Persevere
and Indulge Not,' still another is 'Sub Cruce Veritas '   Ap Adam (first)
came out of the Marches of Wales   Lords of the Marches were noble-
men who, in the early ages, inhabited and secured the Marches of Wales and
Scotland, ruling as if they were petty kings, with their private laws, these
were subsequently abolished '

In connection with the above extract from the "Adams History " the two following letters, written respectively by Mrs Flora Adams Darling and Mrs Leroy Sunderland Smith, of New York, will be of interest

"NEW YORK, May 8, 1895

"*Mrs George B Saunders*

"DEAR MADAM Pardon my seeming neglect in allowing your interesting letter to remain so long unanswered, etc I know we are kindred of a remote degree, all springing from the same ancestral tree, planted in Wales, grafted in Scotland and England Your line, names, dates, events are all correct I refer you to my sister, who is Historian General, United States Daughters, to give you the data, etc There was an article on Ap Adam's pedigree in the 'Daughters of the Revolution,' published 64 Madison Avenue, New York. October, 1894, etc , but, in the 'Historical Register' and other books of peerage, both in this country and England, our ancestress, the daughter of William the Conqueror, is in direct line, through Charles the Bald, to Charlemagne, the great conqueror of the West, but we are willing to rest on Henry, Richard, Thomas and Robert, the founders of the several Adams families in this country and others in the old The study of lineage is not only instructive, but interesting, and your own is specially desirable, united with the Lynch family Such men as Generals Dan and Wirt Adams, proved by deeds they were sons of illustrous sires, and you can proudly continue your work and enjoy the laurels of ancestry "Faithfully,

"FLORA ADAMS DARLING,

"Founder-General Daughters of Revolution "

Mrs Leroy Smith's letter is as follows

"DEAR MADAM My sister, Mrs Darling, requested me to write you what I know of your branch of the Adams family, instead of which I forward you a book containing all I know, etc I shall be pleased to assist you in your researches at any time We have traced our family back in Europe to Charlemagne Hoping the book may be of some service to you, I remain cordially your kinswoman, "SADIE ADAMS SMITH "

Penelope Lynch, wife of Captain Robert Adams, Jr , of the Revolution, was a daughter of Charles Lynch, Sr (the first of his name in Virginia), and his wife, Sarah Clark, the daughter of Christopher and Penelope Clark, of Louisa county, Va. Robert Adams, Jr , had a sister, Judith Adams, born in 1716, and married to Micajah Clark (born 1718), a son of Christopher Clark Besides Judith, there were two more Adams sisters, who married two brothers, Achilles and Charles Moorman, or Moreman, as the name is sometimes spelled There was a third Moorman brother, Thomas, who married Rachel, the daughter of Christopher and Penelope Clark Judith Adams and her hus-

band, Micajah Clark, had among other children a son named Robert Clark,
and his sons moved to Kentucky and became prominent settlers of that state,
Clark county, Ky , is named for them   Among Robert Clark s descendants in
Kentucky, may be mentioned, Governor James Clark, Patterson Clark, Gen
George Rogers Clark, Bennett Clark, Christopher Clark and the Hon John B.
Clark, of Missouri, a son of Bennett Clark.

The "immigrant," Charles Lynch, was thirteen years old when he arrived
in Norfolk   The date of his arrival is not certain, but is said to be anywhere from
1718 to 1720   On attaining manhood he married Sarah, the daughter of his
benefactor, Christopher Clark   The will of Charles Lynch, "the immigrant,"
is on record in Albemarle courthouse and was probated in 1753, the year of
his death   His widow, Sarah Clark Lynch, afterwards married Major John
Ward, of the "Dan river country "   They had no children, and their marriage
license is recorded in Bedford courthouse, and is issued to John Ward, widower,
and Sarah Lynch, widow, December 17, 1766   It is an odd coincidence that
Christopher, son of Major Charles Lynch and Sarah Clark, should have married
Anne Ward, daughter of Major John Ward, just about a year before his
mother was married to his father-in-law   The license is issued to "Christopher Lynch, bachelor, and Anne Ward, spinster, October 15, 1765 "   Charles
and Sarah Clark Lynch had the following family, viz

1 Penelope Lynch who married Captain Robert Adams, Jr., of the
   Revolution
2 Colonel Charles Lynch, of the Revolution, the sponsor of "lynch law"
   (born in 1736, died 1796) who married Anna Terrell, the daughter
   of Henry Terrell (first)   She was born in 1739, and died 1804.
3 John Lynch, the founder of Lynchburg, Va , who married Miss Mary
   Bowles
4 Sarah Lynch, who married Micajah Terrell
5. Christopher Lynch, who married Anne Ward, and had but one child,
   Penelope, who died in infancy

Major Charles Lynch (husband of Sarah Clark) was a member of the House
of Burgesses from 1747 to 1751, representing the counties of Campbell and
Bedford (see Burke's "History of Virginia," volume third, page 133, and also
volume fourth of same)   Mrs. Cabell in "Sketches and Recollections of
Lynchburg," says   "Mr Lynch represented the counties of Campbell and
Bedford in the House of Burgesses, which then sat at Williamsburg, and he was
elected to that honorable office without his knowledge," etc   "Soon after his
death, on the division of his property, his son John became heir to the spot on
which Lynchburg now stands, and by him it was vested in the hands of trustees
to be laid off in lots for the erection of a town," etc   "Mr Lynch (the
immigrant) was said to possess naturally pleasing and graceful manners   He
married, when quite young, a Miss Clark, a young lady belonging to a wealthy
and prominent family   It may not be altogether uninteresting to some to relate

a little incident in connection with this lady   Miss Clark and three other sisters
married about the same time   Each of these sisters received on her marriage
half a dozen silver spoons   As may be imagined, silver spoons were rare
articles in the British Colonies   One of these spoons has descended and is now
in the possession of one of the family, who keeps it as a precious relic of the
past   It has been stated in an extract from the St Louis Republican that
Mr Lynch took up a large body of land on the James river, in sight of the
Peaks of Otter   He made his home at Chestnut Hill, just below Lynchburg,
which place was afterward owned by Judge Edmond Winston, whose family
was also connected and related to the Clark family into which Mr Lynch
married "

The above extracts are taken from Sketches and Recollections of Lynchburg, published by C H Wynne, of Richmond in 1858, and written by Mrs
Cabell, whose maiden name was Mary Anna Anthony, and who was a lineal
descendant of Christopher Clark, through his daughter, who married an
Anthony   The Clark family were of English descent   It is not known
exactly when they came to America, but it is probable that they came by way
of Barbadoes, for in the list of inhabitants of Christ Church Parish, Barbadoes,
in 1680, appear the names of Christopher, Francis, Thomas and Edward Clark
as land and slave owners   It is very probable that the Clarks who settled in
the West Indies, emigrated thence to Virginia, especially as the family names
are the same. In 1705 and 1706, we find in the land records of Virginia, one
Christopher Clark, buying lands on Cedar creek, Hanover county, probably the
father of Christopher, whose daughter Sarah married Charles Lynch—"the
immigrant "   The Clark and Moorman families came to Virginia about the
same time, and settled first in the same locality, they were friends, and some
think relatives, in England before they emigrated   There were many intermarriages between the two families in Virginia   There are two traditions in
regard to the first Moormans one is that Charles Moorman, the progenitor of
the family in the United States, came from England, bringing his sons Thomas,
Achilles, Charles and Robert with him, and settled at Green Springs in Louisa
county, Virginia, the other is that Thomas Achilles and Charles Moorman,
brothers, came from England and settled in Albemarle county   These three
Moorman brothers were among the first settlers in Albemarle, and there is a
stream of some size in that county called "Moorman's river" to this day
Thomas Moorman married Rachael Clark, daughter of Christopher and Penelope
Clark, and Achilles and Charles Moorman each married a sister of Captain
"Robin" or Robert Adams, Jr , and the third Adams sister, Judith, married
Micajah Clark, the son of Christopher and the brother of Rachael Clark, wife of
Thomas Moorman

The will of Christopher Clark is on record in Louisa county, dated August
14, 1741, and proved May 28, 1754   The legatees are Daughters, Agnes
Johnson, Rachel Moorman, Sarah Lynch, sons Micajah Bowling and Edward

Clark, granddaughter, Penelope Lynch (afterwards wife of Robert Adams, Jr),
and wife Penelope Clark.   To his son Edward he willed, "my trooping arms,
my great Bible, and all my law books '   Christopher Clark was captain of a
company of troopers in the French and Indian wars and it is evident that the
"trooping arms ' bequeathed to his son Edward were relics of that war. It has
so far been impossible to definitely settle the question of the family name of
Christopher Clark's wife, Penelope. There is a strong supposition, however,
that she was a Massie and these Massies were kin to the Benjamin Johnson
who married Christopher Clark's daughter, Agnes, both Massies and Johnsons
are said to be lineal descendants of the Earl of Shaftesbury, the former proprietor of the Carolinas, and the one who named Charleston for King Charles
of England, and gave to the two rivers near it his own family names of Ashley
and Cooper   Gershom Perdue, the "Venerable Quaker," says that Christopher
Clark's daughter, Agnes, married "Benjamin Johnson, the son of Sir Andrew
Johnson, a Scotchman," and alludes to these Johnsons, as "an ancient family of
Friends of high descent, from Scotland "

The arms of the Lynches of Galway, and of the Virginia Lynches, are as
follows   Shield, azure, on which is a design of a chevron between three trefoil
leaves, argent, crest, a lynx, passant guardant, motto, "Semper Fidelis "
There is a pretty tradition regarding the origin of the Lynch arms   It is said,
that in olden days, an ancestor defended a castle or town so bravely and
determinedly, that provisions giving out, rather than surrender he forced his
garrison to eat trefoil leaves. His bravery won the day, and in recognition of
his services he was knighted by his sovereign, who gave him the above as his
coat of arms   Mention is made of the Lynches in Hardiman's "History of
Galway," in Haverty's "Irish-American Almanac,' and in John Burke s
"History of Virginia " Burke says (volume third, page 133)   "The new
Assembly met, agreeably to prorogation, on the third of November (1748) '
By an inspection it will be seen that it contained some of the most respectable
names in Virginia Note   The following is a list of the Burgesses elected from
the several counties to serve in the present General Assembly, viz   For
Accomac, Thomas Parramore. Edward Allen, Albemarle, Joshua Fry, Charles
Lynch, etc (this was Major Charles Lynch, the immigrant)   The following
extracts, taken from "The Cabells and Their Kin,' by Alexander Brown, are
of importance, as they contain much valuable information concerning the allied
families of Adams, Lynch, Clark, etc   On page 48, is this bit of information
"The first Court of Albemarle County met January 24, 1744, to February 4,
1745   The records are not complete, the court minutes between 1748 and
1783, a very important period, are missing   The first justices were, Joshua
Fry, presiding, William Cabell, etc, Charles Lynch, etc   On page 49,
"Among the first sheriffs is mentioned Charles Lynch, 1749 to 1751 "   "June
Court, 1745—William Cabell, Charles Lynch and others, produced commissions
from the governor as captains and took the usual oath   ' August Court,

1745—Charles Lynch given leave to keep a ferry from his land across the North river (Rivanna) to the opposite side, William Cabell his security "

Page 69 has the following "In 1749 a meeting (i e. Quaker meeting) was settled near the Sugar Loaf mountains, with Christopher Clark, Sr , and Bowling Clark as overseers This meeting (then in Louisa) was in the present Albemarle, near Stony Point The road between the Camp Creek Quakers and the Sugar Loaf mountains was called "Clark's Track," it went across Machump's creek, through the gap in the southeast mountains, between Castle Hill and Grace Church The Clarks were among the first settlers beyond the Chestnut mountains " Tenth, 8th month, 1754, Friends at South River in Albemarle, petition that they have a meeting established among them It was granted on the 12th of the 10th month, 1754, and Bowlen and Edward Clark were appointed overseers of the week-day meeting, at South River This meeting was south of the river (some three or four miles south of the present Lynchburg), on Lynch's Creek, of Blackwater It was then in Albemarle, but after January first following, in old Bedford (now Campbell) county It was located on the land of Mrs Sarah Lynch (sister of Bowlen and Edward Clark, the overseers), widow of Major Charles Lynch, the emigrant, some time burgess from Albemarle for whom Lynch's river was named He was not a Quaker His wife, a daughter of Christopher Clark, Sr (one of the first overseers of Sugar Loaf meeting), joined the society in 1750, about which time he removed from his former home near Lynch's Ferry, on the Rivanna (North Fork), and settled on his lands near the future Lynch's Ferry, on the Fluvanna (the South Fork of James river), where he died in 1753 His widow qualified as executrix of his will May 10th, 1753, with John Anthony, William Cabell and Joseph Anthony as her securities Joseph Anthony was her brother-in-law Her son, John Lynch, then about fourteen years old, was afterwards the founder of Lynchburg

On page 71, is this "Among the first of the leading men to leave (the Quakers), was Charles Lynch, Jr., one of the founders of the South River meeting, and clerk of that meeting from 15th of July, 1758, to about 1767, when he left the society and afterwards became a Colonel in the Revolutionary army " On page 321 we find that Christopher Anthony, Sr , "moved to Cincinnati, Ohio, about 1814, and died there October 28, 1815. He was a son of Joseph Anthony, by his wife, Elizabeth Clark (sister to Edward, Bowling and Micajah Clark, and to the wives of Benjamin Johnson, Thomas Moorman and Charles Lynch, Sr.), daughter of Christopher Clark, of Louisa county, who, on June 16, 1722, in partnership with Nicholas Merewether, patented 972 acres in Hanover. From 1722 to 1739, he patented 4,926 acres in his own name in the same county " "In 1742 he was one of the first justices of Louisa county " " In the will of Nicholas Merewether (dated December 12, 1743), he is called Captain," etc " He was not an original Quaker, but joined the society between 1743 and 1746 " On page 38 we find that, "in 1741, Wade Netherlands,

6

Richard Mosby, etc , Charles Lynch, etc., were justices of the peace for the
county of Goochland (formed in 1728) " On page 47, "The first court (of
Louisa county) was held on December 13 to 24, 1742, with the following
justices   Robert Lewis, presiding, Christopher Clark," etc , "gents " On
page 366, we find that, "in 1780, co-operating with Colonel William Preston,
Colonel Charles Lynch, Captain Robert Adams, Jr , and other faithful citizens,
he (Colonel James Callaway) suppressed a conspiracy against the commonwealth, by measures 'not strictly warranted by law, although justifiable from
the imminence of the danger.' (See Hening's Statutes of Virginia)   The
conspirators (Tories) were tried before a sort of drum-head court martial,
Colonel Charles Lynch acting as judge, and were condemned to be punished
in various ways   This was the origin in our statutes of the term lynch law "
The above extracts, all taken from the "Cabells and their Kin, ' are of more
than usual interest, from the fact that that book was written by Mr Alexander
Brown, who is generally conceded to be one of the best informed of the genealogists and historians of this day in Virginia   Mr Brown's wife is also a
lineal descendant of Christopher Clark, Sr.

As "lynch law" has become, in our day, one of the problems of the
century, it will be best to give a more full and detailed account of what it really
was in its inception, and how Colonel Charles Lynch's name came to be used in
connection with it   The following article on this subject was written by Robert
W. Carroll, and published first in the Chicago "Inter Ocean," and afterwards
in the Atlanta "Constitution," of December 30th, 1888

"A name or term often takes hold on the popular imagination, and when
by general or continued use it is admitted to hold a place in the language, its
origin has a certain interest, and is at least entitled to historical fairness in its
investigation   Of such is the term 'lynch law,' now constantly heard wherever
the English language is spoken   The modern dictionaries have accepted it,
giving it a definition and even a local origin, and some of the encyclopædias have
treated it as entitled to notice   Possibly its birth ought to be well known , but
there seems to be a lack of exact information on the subject   An article from
your columns, partly devoted to 'lynch law,' is going the rounds of the
newspapers, and it may serve me with an excuse for intruding on you with an
attempt to state facts

"Your contributor wrote from Lynchburg, Va , and ascribed the source
of the term to one John Lynch, whom he represented as having owned a ferry at
the site of Lynchburg, as having got a commission as justice of the peace, as
having summarily tried horse thieves, and as having, after conviction, sent the
criminals off in the custody of constables, with the understanding that they were
to be hung to the first convenient tree, when fairly out of sight of the court
This account is not correct as to the person whose name will go down to posterity, in this connection, nor as to the manner of procedure   John Lynch
inherited from his father the site of Lynchburg, then a ferry crossing of James

river, and in 1786, founded the present city, where he lived till 1821, when he
died, respected and beloved by all who knew him   Instead of being a man
likely to use such bloody methods of punishments as are attributed to him, he
was an exemplary member of the Society of Friends, whose fundamental teach-
ing was 'Glory to God in the highest, and on earth, peace and good will
towards men,' and which under all circumstances held human life sacred   He
lived and died a Quaker, a gentle, humble man of peace, guiltless of the blood
of any human being   None of the earlier English lexicographers, such as
Johnson, Walker, Richardson and Boag, give the term 'lynch law' or the word
'lynched'   Webster and Worcester define both, whilst Craig, Edinburgh edition
of 1859, has 'to lynch,' and characterizes it as an Americanism.   Webster's
definition of 'lynch law' is, the practice of punishing men for crimes by 'private,
unauthorized persons, without a legal trial', adding, 'the term is said to be derived from a Virginia farmer who thus took the law into his own hands '
Worcester has the same, while Nuttall, London edition, falls into the error of
naming the Virginia farmer John Lynch   From the time Cain slew Abel, men
have, without the forms of law, taken punishment into their own unauthorized
hands, dealing it to others, as whim, or passion, or revenge, or imagined neces-
sity may have suggested   Often these outbursts have been organized efforts,
possessing a certain judicial character, and sometimes they have protected
society when official action has failed, as in the punishment of gamblers at
Natchez and San Francisco, and when a burst of patriotic fury resulted in
emptying British imported tea into Boston harbor, the spirit of liberty was
aroused throughout the colonies   But such organizations as the 'Kuklux,' the
'Mollie Maguires,' and the 'White Caps,' have not been disinterested or necessary, rather, the result of combinations to terrorize or drive out the weak and
unprotected   A designation of this method of illegal action, other than that of
mob law, has seldom been used   In a part of England, many centuries ago,
it was called 'Lydford Law,' but that never became more than a local term,
a Devonshire poet wrote of it

> " 'I have oft heard of Lydford law,
> How in the morn they hang and draw,
> And sit in judgment after ' "

' A castle on the hill was mentioned, where accused persons were imprisoned
till trial, which does not seem to have been an inviting place to sojourn

> " 'To be therein, one might, 'tis guessed,
> 'T were better to be stoned and pressed,
> Or hanged   now choose you whether '

"Some people preferred ' to hang out of the way, than tarry for a trial
Lydford Law, by this, appears to have been a boon accepted, if not administered, as a merciful shortening of suffering   It was provincial and failed to be
recognized at the hands of the lexicographers, whilst 'lynch law,' though
originally provincial has been accepted of all men. The Encyclopædia Brit-

annica alludes to the claim that the term originated from the deeds of a Virginia farmer, but intimates that it may be traced back to the act of James
Fitzstephen Lynch, mayor of Galway, Ireland, in 1493, 'who is said to have
hanged his own son out of the window for defrauding and killing strangers,
without martial or common law, to show a good example to posterity' The
most authentic account of this event is to be found in Hardiman's History of
Galway, and in Hoverty's Irish–American Almanac, and it ignores the theory
of illegal punishment. Had the term originated then and there, it would naturally have appeared in the early dictionaries, and would not have been described as of American origin The facts given by Hardiman, are, in sub-
stance, as follows The mayor was visited at his home in Galway by the son
of a gentleman whose hospitality he had enjoyed in Spain His son, Walter
Lynch, was betrothed to a young lady of Galway Walter became suspicious
of the attentions of the Spaniard to his lady-love, and, in a fit of jealous rage,
struck a poignard to his heart and plunged his body into the sea 'In a few
days,' proceeds the chronicle, 'the trial of Walter Lynch took place, a father
was beheld sitting in judgment, like another Brutus, on his only child, and like
him too, condemning that son to die, as a sacrifice to public justice.' Though
the sympathy of the citizens had now turned in favor of the son, and every
effort was made, even to popular tumult, to effect his pardon, the father 'un-
dauntedly declared that the law should take its course' The mayor assisted
the executioner to lead the culprit towards the place of punishment, but they
were impeded by the appearance of a mob, led by members of the mother's
family, demanding mercy. Finding he could not 'accomplish the ends of justice at the accustomed place and by the usual hands, he, by a desperate victory
over parental feeling, resolved himself to perform the sacrifice which he had
vowed to pay on its altar' Still retaining a hold of his unfortunate son, he
mounted with him, by a winding stair within the building that led to an arched
window overlooking the street, which he saw filled with the populace Here
he secured the end of the rope which he previously fixed around the neck of
his son, to an iron staple, which projected from the wall, and, after taking from
him a last embrace, he launched him into eternity The people, 'overawed
by the magnanimous act, retired slowly and peacefully to their several dwell-
ings' The house is said to be yet standing in Lombard street, which is now
known by the name of 'Dead Man's Lane' Over the front doorway are to
be seen a skull and cross-bones executed in black marble, with the motto
'Remember Deathe, Vanitie of Vanities, and All is but Vanities' However
we may admire or condemn the stern sense of justice and hospitality, which
led this Irish father to administer the law upon his own son, it can not be said
that the punishment was inflicted by 'private, unauthorized persons, without
a legal trial' On the contrary it was the infliction of a legal penalty, by an
authorized official, after a regular trial, and in the teeth of a popular clamor
Although the term 'lynch law' did not become a part of the language by

reason of this act, it did originate in the actions of a descendant of the Lynches of Galway, of which the mayor, was, at that time, a prominent representative According to Hardiman and D Alton, the Lynch family came to Ireland with the first English invaders, over six hundred and eighty years ago A younger son migrated westward, to Galway, 'where his line acquired much property, and until the middle of the seventeenth century, was one of its most influential families ' Pence Lynch was the first mayor of Galway, 1184, and during the next two hundred years, no less than eighty-four mayors were Lynches Of this ancient stock was Charles Lynch, the progenitor of the Virginia family of that name Early in the eighteenth century, as a truant schoolboy, he was punished by his mother and sent back to his books Not fancying the prospect of further discipline at the hands of his teacher, he went aboard a vessel just ready to sail for the new world, and was soon afloat on the rough Atlantic, without money and without friends On arriving out, the captain, as was the custom in those days, put the Irish boy up for sale to the highest bidder, to work out his passage money. His bright appearance and the story of his adventure, attracted the attention and moved the sympathy of Christopher Clark, a rich Virginia planter, who bought his services and took him home He was treated as a son, and grew up to manhood, developing ability and unusual energy He made use of his opportunities in cultivating the affections of Sarah Clark, the daughter of his protector, whom, in the course of time, he married They settled in Albemarle county

"Charles Lynch, the immigrant, accumulated land rapidly, some of it on the James river at the present site of Lynchburg, and some of it on the Staunton In its distribution the James river property fell to the lot of John Lynch, whilst that on the Staunton was set off to Charles Lynch, who settled upon its broad acres and lived the life of a rich planter in the midst of his family and slaves

"From 1725 to the period of the Revolution, Quakerism made rapid progress in Virginia, thriving, as usual, under persecution Among the converts were the Clark, Terrell and Lynch families Sarah Clark Lynch carried her children with her into the society, and organized in her own house, and with her family only, the first Quaker meeting near 'Lynch's Ferry '—a meeting that afterwards expanded into large proportions Charles Lynch, second of the same, from the date of his marriage, in 1755, was an active and influential member of the Society of Friends during ten years, being most of the time clerk of the monthly meeting Whatever may have been the process of decline, as the Quakers doubtless thought it, he became 'unsatisfactory' to the society, and in 1767 was disowned for 'taking solemn oaths, contrary to the order and discipline of Friends,' as the minutes of the meeting express it Though Charles Lynch ceased to be a Quaker, he did not lose the leading position among the people of his section of Virginia, which his ability and force of character had secured. From the beginning of the controversy between the colonies and England he was an ardent Whig patriot. When the Revolution broke out he naturally and easily came to the front as a leader While the majority of the people were patriotic Whigs, there were yet many Tories who sympathized with and sustained the English government and confidently counted on the failure of the revolt As in all disturbed conditions of society, the worthless and dishonest and criminal classes came to the surface to add to the confusion and strife which afflicted the country Generally these tories and outlaws were dealt with by voluntary organizations of counties, or towns or neighborhoods In the sparsely settled region of Virginia, near the mountains, tories, tramps, horse thieves and other outlaws abounded, and there were no courts or other legal organizations capable of dealing with them Having repudiated allegiance to England, it was by slow degrees that the Revolutionary government could supply the necessary local organizations In this emergency, Charles Lynch took his place at the head of the Whig party in his section of the colony, and proceeded to suppress lawlessness without the authority of law, and indeed, without asking the people around him for permission to represent them He was so eminently a leader and so efficient in his operations, that scarcely any names are mentioned in this connection save his How it happened that a plain planter in this remote district of country, so vividly impressed the popular imagination that his name became identified, probably for all time, with mob violence, can only be explained on the theory that his methods were striking, and his individuality pronounced and picturesque. What his course of procedure was, is not clearly known, as there were no contemporaneous newspaper writers to report the trials at which he presided. In 1844, Howe's 'Historical Collections of Virginia,' made a record of the accepted legends of that period, and soon after, 'Recollections of Lynchburg' substantially gave the same narrative The traditions of the Lynch family and the immediate neighborhood fairly agree with these more formal historical references, but they contain more details These traditions are that Charles Lynch and two neighbors, Robert Adams, Jr., and James Callaway, all men of wealth and influence, took it upon themselves to protect society and support the Revolutionary government in the region of Staunton river. Charles Lynch had a band of men in his special service, who were sent out by him into the various parts of the country to overawe the Tories, and bring in for trial anyone accused or suspected of correspondence with the enemy, or of acts subversive of social order Trials were held at the residence of Colonel Lynch, on the Staunton river, who uniformly presided as judge, with Captains Adams and Callaway as his associates and advisers The alleged culprit was brought face to face with his accuser, heard the testimony against him and was permitted to call witnesses, and be heard in his own defense If acquitted, he was let go, often with apologies and reparation If convicted, sentence followed promptly, and punishment was summarily inflicted, there being no higher court to interpose the law's delay Stripes on the bare back, or banishment or both, closed the scene However, those found guilty of blatant disloyalty to the Continental Congress, were whipped and then suspended by the thumbs, until they shouted, 'Liberty forever!' the latter penalty indicating a sentimental fervor of patriotism in the heart of the judge A walnut tree growing in the corner of Colonel Lynch's yard was the place of execution, and many a 'Tory' hung by his thumbs to its spreading boughs, until he recanted his disloyalty The residence, which stood about two miles from 'Lynch station,' was burned down a few years ago, but the venerable walnut tree escaped destruction, and yet lives, the dumb witness of the doom of many Tories and outlaws Although 'lynch law' is associated in the popular mind with the idea of the death penalty, yet it is a curious fact that in no instance was the culprit condemned to die by the original Judge Lynch This remarkable exemption was clearly the result of the strain of Quakerism, which no wordly association had yet been able to eradicate As the war progressed, Charles Lynch so far left behind him the principles of his early life, as to raise and command a regiment of riflemen He joined the army of General Greene, himself a scion of Quaker stock then dodging Lord Cornwallis through North and South Carolina

"At the battle of Guilford Court House, fought March 15 1781, Colonel Lynch's regiment, reduced to two hundred men held position on the right flank of Greene's army and did gallant service Not long after the war closed, Colonel Lynch died, leaving a large estate and the savor of a good name to his family He was buried in the graveyard on his homestead plantation, and the following inscription is found on his tombstone 'In memory of Colonel Charles Lynch, a zealous and active patriot, died October 29, 1796, aged sixty years' The descendants of Charles Lynch's neighbors, as well as his family, recognize him as the Lynch who gave a name to mob law An old song relating to the deeds of Lynch, Adams and Callaway, is still remembered and repeated in part, by some of the old people of Campbell county The refrain was

"'Hurrah for Colonel Lynch, Captains Bob and Callaway,
They never turned a Tory loose until he shouted, Liberty!'

'I am indebted to Judge Ward, of Lynch's Station, for some of the traditions mentioned, and for the extract from the old song He says 'It goes without doubt, by nearly everybody in this section of Campbell county, that Colonel Charles Lynch was the founder of the lynch law It has been handed down from sire to son, in this part of the country for generations, and they all believe it as much as they do the history of George Washington, or any other known character of the Revolution ' One grandson of Colonel Charles Lynch, fourth of the name in this country, became governor of the territory of Mississippi (he was governor from 1836 to 1838), but the male line of descent is now extinct Though the original immigrant from Galway has innumerable descendants living, Miss Mary Lynch, of Covington, Ky, is the only one of them bearing the name of Lynch She is the granddaughter of the gentle John

Lynch—founder of Lynchburg—whose name, has, by some authorities, been incorrectly substituted for that of his brother, Charles, in connection with the term 'lynch law ' '

Colonel Charles Lynch was a member of the House of Burgesses previous to the Revolution In Burke's " History of Virginia " (Volume III , page 135) is the following   " The Assembly met May 11, 1769, and passed some resolutions to the effect that the taxation of the colony should be in the hands of the burgesses, and that the trials for treason, felony, etc , should take place in the colony   The next day the Governor (Botetourt) addressed the House of Burgesses as follows   ' I have heard of your resolves, and augur ill of their effects , you have made it my duty to dissolve you, and you are dissolved accordingly '   The members retired to a private house in the city and ' adopted ' a non-importation agreement, which was unanimously ' signed,' and then sent out to the counties for other signatures   Among the number signing were Peyton Randolph, Robert Carter Nicholas, Richard Henry Lee, George Washington, Patrick Henry, Jr , and Charles Lynch "

Colonel Charles Lynch was also a member of the House of Burgesses from 1774 to 1775, and both he and his brother-in-law, " Captain Bob " Adams, Jr , were prominent patriots of the Revolution. In Hening's " Statutes At Large of Virginia," is found the following act, passed October, 1782, reciting that, " in the year 1780, divers evil-disposed persons formed a conspiracy, and did actually attempt to levy war against the commonwealth , and, it being represented to the present General Assembly that William Preston, Robert Adams, Jr , James Callaway and Charles Lynch, and other faithful citizens, aided by detachments of volunteers from different parts of the state, did by timely and effectual measures, suppress such conspiracy , and whereas, the measures taken for that purpose may not be strictly warranted by law, though justifiable from the imminence of the danger, therefore, it was enacted that the persons named, and all other persons concerned, should be fully indemnified and exonerated from all penalties," etc

Robert Adams, Jr , as elsewhere stated, was the son of Robert Adams, Sr., by his wife, Mary Lewis, the daughter of William Lewis, a descendant of one John Lewis, the founder of the Lewis family in Virginia   John Lewis, the immigrant, married the Lady Lynne, a daughter of the Laird of Loch Lynne, Scotland, and their descendants were prominent in the settlement of Augusta county, Va (See Howe's History of Virginia, page 181) Some of the Lewises, after the Revolution, intermarried with the Irvine family. (See " Cabells and Their Kin ") Robert Adams, Sr., and Mary Lewis had a large family   Their sons were named William, James, Joel and Robert, Jr , and they also had three daughters that we know of, viz   Judith (born 1716), who married Micajah Clark, son of Christopher Clark, Sr , and the two remaining daughters married two brothers Moorman, named, respectively Achilles and

Charles. I think these two Mesdames Moorman were named Mary and Margaret, but of this there is no certainty. Robert Adams, Jr., married, as we already know, Penelope Lynch, a daughter of Major Charles Lynch and his wife, Sarah Clark, who was a daughter of Captain Christopher Clark and his wife, Penelope Captain "Robin" Adams, Jr., and Penelope Lynch, his wife, had the following family, viz

1 Charles Lynch Adams, who married Elizabeth Tunstall

2 Robert Adams, who married Mary Terrill, a daughter of Joel Terrill, Jr., and of his wife, Anna Lewis (this Anna Lewis being a daughter of David Lewis and his wife, Anna Terrill hence Joel Terrill, Jr., and his wife, Anna Lewis, were first cousins)

3 James Adams, who married Mary Irvine, daughter of David and Jane Kyle Irvine, of Bedford county, Va., and granddaughter of William Irvine

4 Mildred Adams, who married William Ward

5 Elizabeth Adams, who married Colonel James Deering, of the Revolutionary army, and among their children was a son Colonel James Griffin Deering, who married Mary Anna Lynch (born 1802, died 1892), the daughter of Anselm Lynch and his wife, "the widow, Susan Baldwin, née Miller" Anselm Lynch was son of Colonel Charles Lynch (founder of "lynch law") and of his wife, Anna Terrell Colonel James Griffin Deering and his wife, Mary Anna Lynch, had, among other children, a son, the gallant General James Griffin Deering, who was killed in the Confederate service at the battle of Farmville, Va., and a daughter, Mary Anna Deering, who married Thomas Fauntleroy, of Middlesex county Mrs. Fauntleroy inherited and resides at "Avoca" (at Lynch's Station), the old home of her great-grandfather, Colonel Charles Lynch, of the Revolution, and in her yard is standing, to-day, the leafless trunk of the historic walnut tree, upon which Judge Lynch punished "Tories" in the manner already set forth In the spacious hall at "Avoca" hangs the sword of Colonel Lynch, a relic precious beyond expression to his descendants

6 Sarah Adams, who married her first cousin, Charles Lynch, son of her uncle, Colonel Charles Lynch and Anna Terrill (daughter of Henry Terrill the first) Sarah Adams Lynch and her husband moved to the then territory of Mississippi, and among their children were Charles Lynch, who was Governor of Mississippi from 1836 to 1838, and a daughter, Mildred Lynch, who married Stephen Smith, and had a daughter, Emily Lynch Smith, who became the second wife of her kinsman, Christopher Adams, of Iberville Parish, La., said Christopher being the son of James and Mary Irvine Adams

7. Penelope Adams who married John Shackelford

8 Mourning Adams, who married a Mr McGehee

9 Margaret Adams, who married John Rice Smith, of Virginia

10 Peggy Adams, who married Robert Johnson

11 Judith Adams, who married a Mr White

Margaret Adams and John Rice Smith had a daughter, Mildred Smith, who married Matthew Fluornoy, of Kentucky, and they had a daughter, Sallie Fluornoy, who married Robert J Ward, of Kentucky, and they had two sons and two daughters One of the sons was named "Matthew," and one of the daughters was the famous Kentucky belle and beauty, Sallie Ward, of Louisville Sallie Ward married when quite young Bigelow Lawrence, son of Abbott Lawrence, of Boston, from whom she was divorced, and she afterwards married Dr. Robert W Hunt, and on his death she married Vene Armstrong Being again left a widow, she married George Downs, of Louisville, who survives her. Mrs Downs having died in the summer of 1896, leaving but one child, John W Hunt

Among the distinguished descendants of Captain Robert Adams, Jr , of the Revolution, must be mentioned Generals Daniel and William Wirt Adams, of the Confederacy These two were sons of Judge George Adams, of Jackson, Miss , and his wife Anna Wiessiger, of Louisville, Ky , and Judge George Adams was son of Robert Adams and his wife, Mary Terrill, and grandson of Captain Robert Adams, Jr , and Penelope Lynch The "History of the Adams Family," by Henry Whittmore (while stating incorrectly the descent of Dan and Wirt Adams), has this to say in praise of these two gallant men   "Generals Dan and Wirt Adams were distinguished officers in the Confederate army General Dan Adams commanded in one of the last battles of the war, at Selma, Ala   With jeweled consistency, General Wirt Adams declined a position in the Confederate Cabinet, and rode continuously and fearlessly through the whirlwind of war * * * Handsome as Philip the Fair, he stood six feet in his stirrups, the noblest paladin of the South who rode to war At the court of Philip Augustus, he would have led the nobles, at the court of England he would have led the 'barons,' and, with the Crusaders he would have ridden abreast, with Godfrey of Bouillon or Richard Cœur de Lion. One of the first to step into the arena of strife, at his command the smoke of battle canopied the last scene of the Civil War "

James and Mary Irvine Adams had four children, one daughter and three sons, viz   Penelope Adams, Robert Adams, Christopher Adams, and William Adams Their only daughter, Penelope, married James Terrell, June 16th, 1798 They were married by one Abner Early, and their license is recorded at Campbell County Courthouse, Va They had four sons, and one daughter, viz James Terrell, Robert Adams Terrell, who died in Kaufman county, Texas, and for whom the town of Terrell, Texas, was named, Christopher Terrell, and Susan or Susanna Terrell, who married Henry Carlton, and George Whitfield Terrell, attorney-general of Texas The following notice of the death of

"BELLE-GROVE" IBBERVILLE PARISH, LOUISIANA
Erected and Owned by the Adams and Andrews Families

Robert Adams Terrell, was written by Judge A B Norton, and published in a Dallas, Texas, paper, in May, 1881   "During our absence the reaper, Death, has cut down many of our friends   Henry C Pedigo is no more, Robert A Terrell, 'Old Uncle Bob,' has been gathered in—shocks fully ripe, they were * * * Uncle Bob Terrell was another of our old friends—a friend indeed, there was no equivocation, or disguise, or shadow upon the friendship of Bob Terrell, the old surveyor of Kaufman county, the old Texan, the honest and upright man   Terrell, the flourishing town, is named for him   All of his kin we ever knew were our friends, and with one and all we mingle our tears at his decease "

The following obituary, headed "An Old Settler Gone," appeared in a Texas paper shortly after Robert A Terrell's death (he died March 8th, 1881)

' Another veteran and pioneer of Texas, has passed to the unknown country Captain Robert Adams Terrell, died at his residence in this city, last Tuesday evening. * * *   Much of his early life was spent as a hunter and soldier on the Western frontier, in the Rocky mountains, and in New Mexico, and when the civil contest came, in 1861, he followed the flag of the Confederacy * * * Throughout the war he occupied various positions of trust and honor, and at its close found himself a Major in rank, and returned home, broken in health, and seriously impaired in fortune   * * *   He returned to his old homestead, and to the young city, to which he had given his name

"Captain Terrell was a model of a style of manhood that, unfortunately, is declining in numbers   Uncorrupted and incorruptible in integrity, stern and unyielding in his ideas of virtue, he was firm in his opinions when formed and brave in his manner of expressing them   * * * He has gone out to join the veteran army, whose ranks with us, are constantly diminishing in numbers. With his early associate and friend, John G Moore, whose resting place is near his, he sleeps under the quiet of the stars   It can be said of him that he 'sleeps well ' The deceased was born at Murfreesboro, Tenn , February 22, 1820   His parents immigrated to Boone county, Ky , in 1830, and thence to Booneville, Mo., in 1833   In 1837 he was one of Governor Boggs' juvenile militia to drive the Mormons from Missouri to Nauvoo, Ill , whence they were driven by an incensed people to the Rocky mountains in 1849   In October, 1838, he accompanied his mother to the residence of her brother, ' Kit ' Adams (Christopher Adams, of Belle Grove Plantation), of Iberville Parish, La Through the influence of ' Kit ' Adams he secured a position in the office of General Williams, then surveyor-general of Louisiana   In 1840 he joined his brother, George W Terrell, in Nacogdoches, Texas   When Sam Houston was governor of Tennessee, George W. Terrell had filled the office of attorney-general of that state, and he followed Houston to Texas, and was appointed by him attorney-general of the Republic of Texas   In 1842, Captain Robert Adams Terrell received a commission as a secret agent of the republic to Santa Fe, New Mexico, and joined a caravan for that place, where he spent the winter, and was arrested and imprisoned as a spy   Meeting with Louis Valdies,

an old schoolmate, he was released in 1843 He joined the first party of traders
to the Missouri river, and, when in that section, joined the command of Colonel
Snively and proceeded on the famous Santa Fé expedition In 1846 he was
married to Emily L Love, daughter of Judge Love, of Nacogdoches, and soon
afterwards moved to this county and improved his well-known homestead in
this city The fruits of this marriage were a large family of children, most of
whom now reside in Terrell About the time of his marriage, under the
ministration of the old pioneer preacher Rev J W Fields, he joined the
Methodist Episcopal Church, in which faith he lived and died His first wife
dying soon after the war, he was married again in 1868 to Mrs Amelia Terrell, of
this county, who was the widow of Jonathan W Terrell, likewise an early settler
of Texas, who died in this county in 1861 This wife still survives him "

The Terrells of America are descendants of the old Norman-English family
of Tyrrells, who descend from Sir Walter Tyrrell, knight, who killed King
William Rufus in the New Forest The Tyrrell arms are Argent, within a
bordure, engrailed gules, two chevrons, azure, crest, a peacock s tail issuing from
the mouth of a boar s head couped, erect, supporters, two tigers, reguardant,
motto, "Sans Crainte '

Robert Adams, eldest son of James and Mary Irvine Adams, was drowned,
while a boy, out boating, and his body was never recovered, and their youngest
son, William Adams, married Nancy Chinn, a daughter of Benjamin Chinn, and
a cousin of Judge Thomas Chinn, of Kentucky. William Adams (born December 10, 1784), and Nancy Chinn (born December 11 1785), were married
February 14, 1803, and had seven children, viz Mary J Adams, born January
17, 1804, Christopher Adams. Jr, born October 22, 1805, William Clark and
Lewis Merewether Adams, twins, born June 30, 1809, Benjamin Chinn Adams,
born October 2, 1814, Elizabeth Adams, born August 2, 1817, Penelope Lynch
Adams, born June 15, 1819

William Clark Adams married Eliza S Irby on April 1, 1830 He died at
Shelbyville, Ky, June 24, 1854, leaving a son and three daughters, viz
Benjamin Gaither Adams, who married and has children—Sarah Adams, who
married John Austin Emma Adams, who is unmarried, and Anna Eliza Adams,
who married Mr Picot

Mary J Adams (daughter of William and Nancy Chinn Adams) married
Chamberlin Townsend, April 11, 1825, and their children were William Clark
Townsend, born May 22, 1826, James B Townsend, born January 25, 1829,
and a daughter, Mary J. Townsend, who married John Carroll, June 20, 1836

Lewis Merewether Adams, son of William and Nancy Chinn Adams,
married Elizabeth V. Carroll, April 16, 1833

Elizabeth M Adams (daughter of William and Nancy Chinn Adams)
married Judge Dandridge N Ellis, on December 5, 1833, and died August 2,
1834, leaving no children

Christopher Adams Jr son of William and Nancy Chinn Adams) married

Harriet Gage McCall, June 25, 1834, and had the following family Edward White Adams, Richard McCall Adams, born September 21, 1847, died February 10, 1848, Sitgreaves Adams, born August 11, 1848, Christopher Adams, born October 5, 1850, and died July 21, 1851. Frances Harriet Adams, born July 25, 1841, Elizabeth Ellis Adams, born in 1843

Edward White Adams married Julia Biddle Henderson, second daughter of General James Pinckney Henderson, the first Governor of Texas, and also a United States Senator Miss Henderson was also a granddaughter of John Cox, of Philadelphia, a scion of some of the most prominent families of Pennsylvania Edward White Adams was born in Iberville Parish La, August 25, 1844 He was educated in France, and while there met Miss Henderson, whom he married October 14, 1868 They had two children, Julia Henderson Adams, born at Archachon, near Bordeaux, and James Pinckney Henderson Adams, born April 5, 1879, at Weimar, Saxe-Weimar Edward White Adams, through his mother, was a descendant of the McCalls, of Philadelphia, an old colonial family (one of whose daughters during the Revolution married General Gage of the British army), and of the Bayards, Cadwalladers, Kembles, Sitgreaves and Fishers, of New York and Pennsylvania He died at Brighton, England, May 23, 1891

Benjamin Chinn Adams (son of William and Nancy Chinn Adams) married Caroline Blanks, June 26, 1836, and had four children Charles Lynch Adams, Benjamin Chinn Adams, Samuel Adams and Mary Fort Adams Charles Lynch Adams was born in 1838, and in 1872 married Miss Lelia Tardy, of Virginia, who was also his kinswoman through the following line Her mother was Sallie William Ward, who married Samuel C Tardy And Sallie William Ward was a daughter of John Ward and Tabitha Walden, and a granddaughter of William Ward and Mildred Adams, and this Mildred Adams was the daughter of Penelope Lynch and Captain Robert Adams, Jr, of the Revolution Benjamin Chinn Adams is a prominent attorney, of Grenada Miss He married Miss Dora Chamberlain, of that place, and has three children Harry, Benjamin and Dora Adams. Samuel Adams is unmarried. Mary Fort Adams was married in 1870 to Harry Hildreth Hall, and has three children Edith H Hall, who was married in 1895 to Herbert Lincoln Clark, of Philadelphia, Clinton Hall, born in 1877 and now a student at Princeton, and Mildred Sidney Hall, born in 1883 Harry H Hall is of English descent, and was educated at Heidelberg, Germany

Penelope Lynch Adams, born in 1819, was the youngest child of William and Nancy Chinn Adams Shortly before her birth, William Adams, leaving his family in Kentucky, started out for Louisiana with large sums of money on his person, and with the intention of investing in sugar plantations He reached Louisiana, but after that was never heard of again, there are two theories in regard to his death, one is that the boat on which he embarked was captured on the Mississippi river by Lafitte the pirate who, as usual, murdered and plundered all on board, the other theory is that he, while on the way to Louisiana, changed his mind about settling in that state, and decided, instead, to invest in the island of Martinique, thither he accordingly went and on his arrival there died of yellow fever

Penelope Adams, youngest child of William Adams, married Dr John Stone in 1838, and had the following family Albert Stone, Elizabeth Ellis Stone Louise Stone, Mary Eliza Stone, Caroline Stone, who died in childhood, and John Stone, who also died in childhood Albert Stone died unmarried, Elizabeth Ellis Stone married first a Mr John Hall, and secondly Mr Henry Baker, of New Orleans, who was a gallant Confederate soldier, being a member of the famous Washington Artillery Louise Stone married first Dr Alfred Gourrier, and on his death she married Mr John W Borst, of Luray, Va Mary Eliza Stone married Mr James Andrew Ware, and they have one child, John Stone Ware Christopher Adams, the second son of James Adams and Mary Irvine, was born about 1782. He married first Susan or Susanna Johnson, from Lexington, Ky, but whose family were of old Virginia stock, said to be descended from Sir Andrew Johnson, the Scotchman By this marriage there was only one child who lived, Penelope Lynch Adams, who was born about 1813 to 1814, and who married John Andrews, of Norfolk, Va, afterwards of New Orleans Christopher and Susan Johnson Adams moved to Iberville Parish

Christopher Adams was known in his family as "Kit Adams of the Coast" (the left bank of the Mississippi river from above New Orleans to Baton Rouge, being known as the "German coast" since time out of mind, and commonly called "the coast"), to distinguish him from his cousin, the other "Kit" or Christopher Adams of that day, who lived in Mississippi, and married a Miss Powell of that state This Kit Adams was a son of Robert Adams and Mary Terrell, his wife (who was a daughter of Joel and Anna Lewis Terrell), and a grandson of Captain Robert Adams, Jr of the Revolution, and therefore was first cousin to "Kit Adams of the Coast" Christopher Adams' (of Iberville) second wife was his kinswoman, Emily Lynch Smith, daughter of Stephen Smith and Mildred Lynch of Mississippi, who was a sister of Governor Charles Lynch, of that state, and a daughter of Charles Lynch (son of Colonel Charles Lynch, of the Revolution, and Anna Terrell), and his wife (who was also his cousin), Sarah Adams, the daughter of Captain Robert Adams, Jr, and Penelope Lynch Christopher and Emily Lynch Smith Adams had only one child who lived, Mary Fort Adams, who married John Hagan, of "Indian Camp" plantation, Iberville, in 1848. They had three daughters Mary Fort Hagan, born in 1849, who married, in 1874, Colonel Edmund Beale Briggs, of the Confederate service, and had one son, Edmund Beale Briggs, Jr, born in 1875 Mrs Briggs died February 4, 1877. The other two daughters were Virginia Camp Hagan and Sarah Elizabeth Hagan Mrs. John Hagan died in 1880.

The following letter from Mr Robert W Carroll, of Cincinnati, to Mrs George Saunders, is of interest, as it gives much information concerning the Johnsons, the family of Christopher Adams' first wife

" The probabilities are that the Susan Johnson, who was the wife of Christopher Adams, came of the stock of Benjamin Johnson, who, about 1728, married Agnes, the oldest daughter of 'old' Christopher Clark, he and his wife becoming Quakers The descendants of Benjamin and Agnes Johnson were numerous, and had a habit of intermarrying with the Clarks, Terrells and Lynchs, not to mention the Adamses There was a Robert in this line and possibly he was Susan's father (General Charles E. Brown, of the Benjamin Johnson line, just tells me that there were numerous Robert Johnsons of his line) Susanna was a common name in this line of Benjamin Johnson, and doubtless came from Susanna Terrell, of the era 1675–1730, whose grandson, David (second) so continuously married Johnsons. These Johnsons have always made great claims to high descent, that is, they say they are descended from the Earl of Shaftesbury, who was one of the original proprietors of the Carolinas. Their line is not clear, but it seems to runs thus Benjamin Johnson, who married Agnes, was, so they allege, the son of Sir William Johnson (Gershom Perdue says Sir Andrew Johnson), of a Scotch line, who married a Massie, of Virginia, who was a granddaughter or something of Ashley Cooper, Earl of Shaftesbury The name 'Ashley' is found in this line of Johnsons, indicating that the family believed in their alleged descent The Massie lady was named Penelope Her sister, Lucretia, also married a Johnson, but not a relative of Sir William These two Johnson families both with Massie blood, intermarried with each other, and with Terrells, Clarks, etc Though the connection with Shaftesbury has not been made clear, yet the mere fact that these people so far back believed it, must be given weight

· None of them have been able to clearly fasten on to Shaftesbury Possibly Penelope Clark (wife of old Christopher Clark), got her name from Penelope Massie Johnson, and may have been a relative There are still Virginia Johnsons galore, etc On general principles growing out of the fact that they belonged to the same part of Virginia, I am almost disposed to think they were all of the same family In fact, General Brown says his grandfather, Elisha (or Elijah) Johnson, used to speak of Richard M Johnson, of Kentucky, vice-president of the United States under Van Buren, as a cousin, and I suppose R M J belonged to the line of Johnsons I am about to mention Richard Johnson was one of the justices of the court of Spotsylvania county, Va when it was organized, August 1, 1722, see Rev P Slaughter's 'History of St George's Parish,' pages 4 and 8 This Richard Johnson was born probably as far back as 1680

"In 1739, and afterwards, a Richard Johnson was a vestryman in King and Queen county, and William and Thomas Johnson were vestrymen in Louisa county after 1742 See Bishop Meade's work on the 'Old Churches,' of Virginia

Richard Johnson, late of King and Queen county, by his will, dated December 13, 1733, devised 2,765 acres being 'all his land in Caroline county,' to his nephew, Thomas Johnson, and died soon after   And Thomas Johnson, in April, 1757, was seized of 1,711 acres in Louisa county, bought of Ann Cosby, and William Johnson and Martha, his wife   These facts appear, in an act to dock an entail, in Volume VII , Hening's Statutes, page 157   In 1753 Thomas Johnson was one of the trustees appointed by the General Assembly to clear the Mattapony river (Volume VI , Hening's Statutes, page 394)   In 1740 it appears that Richard Johnson, then deceased, had devised land situated in King William county, to Thomas Johnson, also since deceased, and had devised other lands to Richard and William Johnson, brothers of the said Thomas Johnson   Thomas, when he died, left sons, Nicholas Johnson and Richard Johnson, who were also grandsons of Nicholas Meriwether , and Richard Johnson (doubtless brother of Thomas, above mentioned) had sons, Thomas, Richard and William   Hening's, Volume V , page 114

" In 1742, when Louisa county was set off from Hanover, the first county court was organized December 13 to 24, and among the justices were Christopher Clark and Richard Johnson   See 'Cabells and Their Kin,' page 47 * · + If you find a Nicholas Johnson in your line, it would indicate descent from the Johnson, who married a daughter of Nicholas Merewether , if a Benjamin, then from Benjamin and Agnes," etc.   " Very sincerely yours,

" ROBERT W. CARROLL "

As far as can be ascertained, Susan Johnson descended from one Robert Johnson, of the line of Benjamin and Agnes Johnson   Her family moved to Kentucky, where she was born, and later on her father owned sugar plantations in Attakapas, and near Opelousas, La   A coat of arms found on an old china pitcher belonging to these Johnsons, is as follows · Arms, a shield, in the center of which are two lions, standing erect and holding up a gauntlet or mailed glove, at the base of the shield, lying lengthwise is a fish, and at the top of the shield are three mullets or star-shaped designs having six points , the crest is an arm (from shoulder), uplifted, holding aloft a poignard or cross-hilted dagger , the motto is, " Deo Patriaeque Liber "

Christopher and Susan Johnson Adams were married about 1811 or 1812   Their daughter, Penelope Lynch Adams, was born about 1814, and married John Andrews, of Norfolk, Va , in 1832, and died April 10, 1847   (Mr Andrews was born about 1800, and died in February, 1885, and is buried in the Andrews tomb at Donaldsonville, La)

John Andrews was of English descent and came of Catholic stock, his father being kin to the Howards, of England, and his mother, Katherine Fitzgerald, being a descendant of the Arundels and of the ancient Irish family of Fitzgerald.

Penelope Lynch Adams and John Andrews had the following family ,

1. Emily Lynch Adams (named for Emily Lynch Smith, second wife of Christopher Adams), who married Mr Edward Shiff, of Paris, France, and had one son, Edward, born in 1860, and who died unmarried in New Orleans in April, 1886 Mr. Shiff died in 1860, and in April, 1871, his widow married General James P. Major, of the Confederate service, a distinguished soldier and a remarkably handsome man. There were no children by this marriage, and General Major died in Austin, Texas, in 1877

2. Thomas Francis Andrews, who died, unmarried, at "Belle Grove" in 1863

3 Eliza Virginia Andrews, who never married

4 Katherine Andrews, who died in infancy

5 Penelope Lynch Adams Andrews (born at Belle Grove, November 9, 1839), who married Governor Paul Octave Hebert

6 Angela Lewis Andrews (named for Angela Lewis Conrad, who is buried at Mount Vernon, Va), who married Colonel Malcolm Edward Morse, son of Congressman Isaac Edward Morse, of Louisiana, and his wife, Margaretta Wedistrand The Morses being kindred of the Henry family of Virginia, the old English family of 'Cranford," and of the Nicholls family of Louisiana, of which ex-Governor Francis T. Nicholls is a distinguished member The Wedistrands are of Norwegian extraction, descending from "King Harold Blue-Tooth" of Norway Isaac Edward Morse was also Attorney-General of Louisiana when Paul O Hebert was Governor of that state Colonel Malcolm E Morse was a gallant Confederate soldier He died at Baltimore in June, 1895 Angela Lewis Andrews and Colonel Morse had but one child, Angela Lewis Morse, who married her first cousin, Paul Octave Hebert, in February, 1890 They have one child, Dorothy Oleveira Hebert, born March 16, 1894

7 Katherine Andrews, who married Captain Charles Knowlton, of the Confederate service Captain Knowlton is of Northern and Revolutionary stock—his great-grandfather having been a soldier in Washington's army and a member of the "Order of the Cincinnati " There were two children by this marriage, Charles Andrews Knowlton, who was married in 1895 to Florence Osmond, of Cincinnati, Ohio, and who has a child, Charles Osmond Knowlton, born in 1896, and Katherine I. Knowlton, who married Mr Lawrence Mercer, of Montreal, Canada, and had a child, Gladys Katherine Mercer

Governor Hebert and Penelope Lynch Adams Andrews were married at the Jesuits' Church, New Orleans, August 3, 1861, by the Reverend Father Booker, ex-Governor Hebert, being at that time, a Brigadier General in the Confederate service, in command of New Orleans and the defenses of the Gulf He was a who wi in tr t r l t l u c c Will c lu daughter of

Thomas Cabell Vaughan, and his wife, Harriet Letitia Kirkland Wynne, of
Mississippi   Thomas Cabell Vaughan was a descendant of the Willses, Cabells
and Vaughans of Virginia   Thomas Cabell Vaughan Hebert, Governor
Hebert's eldest son by his first marriage, died in the Confederate service, at
Galveston, Texas, 1862   General Paul Octave Hebert was the eldest son of
Paul Gaston Hebert (born at " Plaisance Plantation," Iberville, February 1, 1796,
died May 4, 1852), and of Mary Eugenia Hamilton (born February 27, 1797,
and died September 20, 1843), who was the daughter of Ignatius Hamilton
and his wife, Ann Bush, whom he married in 1787   Ignatius Hamilton was
born in Maryland and emigrated to Louisiana, and was the only child of Joseph
Hamilton, a Scotchman, by his wife, Mary Eugenia Coumbe (or Coombe), of
St Mary's county, Maryland. These Coombes were early settlers of Maryland, and of an old Saxon English family. Anne Bush, wife of Ignatius Hamilton, was a daughter of Daniel Bush, a Virginian, who emigrated to Kentucky
and thence to Louisiana   Joseph Hamilton "the Scotchman" was a descendant of the "Clan Hamilton" that had the famous feud with the "Clan Boyd"
in Scottish history   The Hamilton crest is a tree trunk, with a saw in it, and
the motto, " Through "

Paul G Hebert was justice of the peace for his native parish of Iberville,
a planter and a civil engineer, and a member of the Convention of 1842   He
was the son of Armand Valery Hebert (born March 27, 1753, and died August
28, 1817), and his wife, Marie Celeste Boudreaux (born April 10, 1757, and
died August 12, 1847), who was a daughter of Benjamin Boudreaux (or
Boudraut) and his wife, Cecile Celeste de Melançon

Armand Valery Hebert was a son of Paul Gaston Hebert (born April 13,
1712, and died July 25, 1805), and of his wife, Marguerite Josephine de
Melançon, who was born in Port Royal, Nov 1, 1717

This Paul Gaston was a great-great-grandson of Louis Hebert, who came
from Normandy, France, in 1604, with the Chevaliers de Monts and Cham-
plain and aided in founding Port Royal, the first permanent French colony in
America   The original cause of his leaving France was the persecution to
which the Catholics were subjected in the early part of the reign of Henry of
Navarre, the Huguenot   The Heberts were descendants of an ancient Norman
family, the name "Herbert" is said to be a corruption of their name   They
have always been Catholics, and have a tradition that they got the faith when
Rollo and his pirates were converted from the heathen faith of Norway   The
first American ancestor of the family, who came over in 1604, brought with
him some jewelry of ancient workmanship, and some Norman silver coins
These coins were afterwards melted and moulded into spoons by one of his
descendants, and are held as valued relics in the family to-day, the jewelry
was preserved until the late war   At that time it was in the possession of
Governor Hebert's eldest sister, Marie Evelina, then the wife of Robert Henry
Fenwick Sewall, of Maryland

Mrs Sewall's plantation was in the line of Banks' raid along the Mississippi river, and her house was plundered by stragglers from Banks' army, and she lost her much-prized jewelry, as well as everything else of value, which she possessed

Paul Gaston Hebert, born in 1712, was the first of his name in Louisiana, and he was the one who burned down his house and other buildings in Port Royal, in the face of British troops, rather than take the oath of allegiance to the English crown, or submit to the religious restrictions which the Church of England was endeavoring at that time to place upon Catholic worship and observances   He left Port Royal, October 28, 1755, sojourned in New England from March 7, 1756 to July 28, 1767, when he went to Louisiana   He was one of the earliest permanent settlers of the parish of Iberville   His son, Armand Valery Hebert, ranked as a major in the French provincial army of Louisiana, and was a member of the old "constitutional convention of 1812," which met to revise the laws of Louisiana after that province had been sold by Napoleon to the United States   His grandson, Paul Hebert, was a member of the Convention of 1842, and his great-grandson, Governor Paul Octave Hebert, was a member of the Convention of 1852   The "Statesman," a New Orleans paper, of Saturday, January 6, 1855, has the following·   "Governor Hebert is a native of Louisiana   Both he and his parents were born in the state which has called him to its highest office   There are, in the history of this family, some evidences of that stern adhesion to principle which marked the Puritans of Plymouth Rock.   Allegiance was not a thing which with them could be lightly laid aside like an old garment, nor could new rulers find worship merely because they were the representatives of power.   In 1753 his great-grandfather, then a native of Canada, burned his own house to the ground, rather than submit to English tyranny   He abandoned his home and its associations to escape the rule of strangers, and found a new home in our state long before the colonies dreamed of independence   He was one of the earliest permanent settlers of the parish of Iberville   In all the important scenes which have transpired in this state he and his descendants have borne an important part   The grandfather was a member of the constitutional convention of 1812, the grandson, of the convention of 1842, and the great-grandson of the convention of 1852   From father to son has descended that stern independence, that adhesion to principle, which in another sphere made heroes of our fathers and gave birth to a new empire "   The following article accompanied by a steel engraving of Governor Hebert, appeared in a Louisiana magazine of that day

" Paul Octave Hebert, the present Governor of Louisiana, is the youngest person who has ever held that office   He was born December 12, 1818, in the parish of Iberville (on the 'Plaisance Plantation'), in this state, of an old Creole family, and is consequently but thirty-four years old.   Having graduated at Jefferson College, La., when quite a boy, Paul was sent to the West Point Academy, where he remained .... an excellent mathe-

matical head and being apt at all the branches of learning, he soon obtained
an honorable and distinguished position among the graduates, leading several
classes and finally graduating with the highest honors in 1840

"The best graduates of West Point are transferred to the corps of engineers,
and accordingly Paul received a commission as second lieutenant of the corps
of engineers, on July 1, 1840 Shortly afterwards, as a tribute to his excel-
lence and thoroughness as a scholar, he was appointed acting assistant professor
of engineering, in the Military Academy, which post he filled from August 30,
1841, to July 21, 1842 After serving with credit in the corps of engineers,
Lieutenant Hebert yielded to the superior claims of his family and native state,
and resigned his commission in order to be near an aged father, * * * and
also to render that duty which every man owes to his own state—of promoting
and aiding her welfare and safety Louisiana stood in great need of a sensible
and scientific engineer, to guard the immense interests which are constantly
exposed to destruction from causes that need the utmost vigilance to prevent
She had suffered greatly from the ignorance and neglect of those who had
charge of those interests, and the development of her immense resources had
been thus greatly retarded Under these circumstances, the office of state
engineeer was pressed upon the young ex-lieutenant of engineers, in 1845, by
his Excellency Governor A Monton It was accepted, and Hebert entered
upon the duties of the office in 1845, and continued to perform them until 1847.
The state never had an abler engineer ; but, unfortunately, his opinions were not
regarded by the legislature on one very momentous question, and he resigned
the post The subject to which we refer was the proposition to shorten the
distance between this city (New Orleans) and Natchez. by making a cut-off below the mouth of the Red river, that is, by digging a new direct channel for
the river at a point where it commenced a long circuit State Engineer
Hebert remonstrated against this measure, and demonstrated most clearly that
it would derange the whole order of the stream, and produce numerous crevasses,
overflows and other disasters His advice was not heeded. As an evidence of
the sincerity and sagacity of the state engineer, he caused his own house
('White Castle'), which stood near the river bank, to be moved back some
distance, declaring that it would cave in shortly after the cut-off was completed
The fact proved as he predicted and justified his prudence—the river now flows
where the old mansion stood He also resigned the office of surveyor-general,
not wishing that his administration should be remembered by the calamities
from which he had labored in vain to free the state The cut-off was carried
It has justly been regarded as the source of more losses and annoyances to the
residents on the banks of the river below than any event in the history of the
state Ever since then no summer has passed without several most desolating
crevasses, commencing with the terrible one at Sauve's, which inflicted on this
city a loss of several millions On the breaking out of the Mexican War, Hebert
offered his services to the general government and on the organization of the

new ten regiments was appointed lieutenant colonel of the 'Fourteenth,' under the veteran Trousdale   One-half of this regiment was raised in Louisiana.   It commenced service in a brigade commanded by Franklin Pierce, the present President of the United States   It is a notable fact that the commander of this brigade should have been elected President of the United States, and three of the colonels should have been elected governors of states, to wit Seymour of Connecticut, Trousdale of Tennessee, and Hebert of Louisiana

"The 'Fourteenth' greatly distinguished itself in all the actions in which it participated   For young and fresh troops, its officers and men were remarkable for their steadiness, gallantry and efficiency   Much of this was due to the dauntless character of the veteran colonel and the admirable self-possession and skill of the lieutenant-colonel   The regiment was engaged in all the battles of the valley—Contreras, Churubusco, Molino del Rey, Chapultepec and the assault upon the gates of the City of Mexico   Colonel Trousdale being badly wounded at the battle of Chapultepec, while bravely leading a charge against a Mexican battery planted across the road leading to the Garita of San Cosmo, the command devolved upon the lieutenant-colonel, who fulfilled his duties with skill, gallantry and coolness   (Hebert led the 'forlorn hope' which captured Chapultepec) Lieutenant-Colonel Hebert was brevetted a full colonel for gallant conduct at the terrible battle of Molino del Rey, where of five lieutenant-colonels in Worth's command three were killed or mortally wounded—Martin Scott, Graham and McIntosh   On the disbandment of the troops, Colonel Hebert returned to Louisiana with the high commendation of all his superior officers, and particularly of his brigadier-general, Franklin Pierce   (In Pierce's diary kept during the Mexican campaign and published in Nathaniel Hawthorne's 'Life of Pierce,' he makes frequent mention of Hebert, calling him 'the gallant young Creole colonel ') Devoting his mind to the care and improvement of a large plantation, Colonel Hebert remained at home until ill health demanded recreation, change of air, etc , when he made the tour of Europe   Happening in Paris on the 4th of July, he was invited to preside at a banquet given by some Americans, in honor of the day   On this occasion an incident occurred which is worthy of record   It was when Louis Napoleon was carrying into effect his despotic suppression of all public assemblies and demonstrations , patriotic songs, and especially the 'Marseillaise,' were prohibited   Now it happened that at the meeting of Americans to celebrate the independence of their states, there was a very natural desire to hear the 'Marseillaise ' It was therefore called for, when the chief of the band of musicians who attended the dinner, came forward and showed the 'president' the order against playing or singing that revolutionary song   Thereupon Colonel Hebert arose and proposed that, as the law applied only to Frenchmen, the company should sing the hymn themselves   The proposition was received with loud applause, and the colonel leading off, the whole company joined in and executed in a very enthusiastic if not harmonious manner this animated

song of liberty   The old and familiar notes attracted crowds of Frenchmen
around the hall, who joined in the chorus and manifested the liveliest emotions
at a scene suggestive of proud recollections, but which, alas, had become so
rare of late   On his return to the United States Colonel Hebert was elected a
member of the ' convention of 1852, to revise the state Constitution,' from his
old and native Parish of Iberville   In the convention he was prominent for his
devotion to liberal and Democratic principles. His sense of justice and the
consistency of his principles were strikingly displayed in his vote against that
feature of the constitution which included slaves as the basis of representation
The object of the provision was to restrict the representation of New Orleans,
and give greater power and weight to the slave-holding country parishes
Though a country member and a large slave-holder, Colonel Hebert voted
against the provision   In November, 1852, Colonel Hebert was nominated by
the Democracy for governor   After a brief but active canvass he was elected
over his opponent, Louis Bordelon, by a very large majority, the city of New
Orleans alone giving him over twelve hundred majority   The exertion and
fatigue of the canvass produced a dangerous and lingering illness from which
Colonel Hebert did not recover in time to enter actively upon his duties at the
period designated by the Constitution   To give validity, however, to the acts
of legislature, he was inaugurated and sworn into office on his sick bed, at his
residence (White Castle), and Chief Justice Eustis administered the oath,
when he had not the strength to sit up   He recovered, however, in time to
enter upon his duties at the capital, and though he has had no opportunity of
developing the policy of his administration, it is quite obvious that it will be
marked by the characteristics of his mind and temperament as one of progress,
of liberal enterprise and of patriotic devotion to the honor and best interests
of his native state "

    The cut-off referred to in the above article was the famous " Raccourci cut-
off " When Colonel Hebert was a member of the convention of 1852, he voted
in favor of the discontinuance of the French language as the only official language of the courts, legislatures, etc , and advocated the equal use of both
English and French, this step greatly incensed some of the less progressive of
the Creole population, and " L'Abeille," the chief Creole organ, was especially
wrought up over the matter   The following is from a New Orleans paper, of
Wednesday, December 12, 1852   " We refer to the effort to excite jealousies
between Creole and other portions of our population   We protest against all
such attempts   ✻ ✻ ✻ Whatever stock or parentage we spring from, whatever
tongue we speak, we are one people, not Frenchmen, not Creoles, not Anglo-
Saxons, ✻ ✻ ✻ but Americans   The attempt to excite these prejudices of
race ✻ ✻ ✻ has thus far been chiefly through the French side of the ' Bee.'
We unmasked the treacherous design yesterday, by translating a labored edito-
rial from that journal, that those who do not read French may see the trick
that is being played   Aware that they are ' trifling with edged tools,' using a

knife 'that cuts both ways,' they publish in French what they dare not print in English + + ' They talk about Colonel Hebert's hostility to the Creoles and to their progenitors, the French, and they talk as gravely as though they believed it themselves, or fancied anybody else would believe it. But these ingenious gentlemen deceive themselves. They proceed upon the calculation that they can humbug and delude the Creole voters of Louisiana. A futile calculation. There is not a man among us—a scion of the ancient population—who does not know Hebert and appreciate the sympathies, the pride of descent, the attachment to his native soil and the national patriotism which warm and animate his bosom. The very men who now say to the descendants of Frenchmen, 'Vote against Hebert, he is ashamed of you and of your language,' go above Canal street and say to the Anglo Saxon and naturalized portion of our population, 'vote against Hebert, he is a *Creole*, his ancestors were *French!*' It is but a repetition of the deceitful and disgraceful tactics which they employed against Gen. Pierce, when they printed pamphlets *in the South* and sent them *North*, representing that he had always stood up for Southern rights and voted in defense of slavery, and the same committee printed pamphlets and suborned witnesses, like Fogg and Foss and other vile abolitionists, to swear that Pierce concurred with them, and with these they flooded the *South!* And this is the game they are playing against Hebert. On one side of Canal street, where the generous Creole sons of Louisiana are numerous, and all along the coast they appeal to their susceptibilities and pride of race, and say, 'This man is faithless to you, he has been adopted by the Irish, Germans and Anglo-Saxons.' And, on the other side of Canal street and in the upper parishes Whig agents are sneaking into every coffee-house and crossroad tavern, crying out, 'Down with Hebert, he is one of those ambitious, grasping Creoles, that are after everything, he has no American feeling like Bordelon.'"

The following is from a New Orleans paper of December 12, 1852. "One of the most original thinkers that ever appeared in Louisiana—the late Isaac T. Preston, a man whose memory will long be honored by a people to whom he was devoted—in the last great speech which he made in the legislature on a 'bill to protect New Orleans from inundation,' after quoting Colonel Hebert's 'Report' (when state engineer), thus refers to him. 'Great and gallant soul! You were allured from this mighty scheme to join in the conquest of Mexico. You acquired a glory as brilliant as that which encircled the brow of any other hero in that unparalleled achievement. But your laurels, with all the dust of California secured by the conquest, are but as trash compared with the acme of health, wealth illimitable and never-ending prosperity, happiness and glory, which you have pointed out for your own, your native land. May you and the statesmen and patriots of Louisiana, pursue its attainment with all the energy of your glowing recommendations.' This is high encomium indeed, when we consider that it was applied to a very young man, by one of the oldest and most enlightened of the jurists and statesmen of Louisiana—a man whose fertile mind scarcely ever, unless in this single instance, accepted ideas or suggestions from others "

In 1855 Governor Hebert ran in opposition to John Slidell for the Democratic nomination for the United States senatorship, but finally withdrew his name of his own accord rather than risk a split in the party, and the consequent election of a Whig candidate   The " Louisiana State Republican," a Whig paper, of January 10 1855, has the following   "The canvass for the United States senatorship is waxing warm   The friends of the respective candidates, and there are now only two prominently before the people, * * * are pushing their claims with earnestness and zeal   The names of these distinguished gentlemen are Governor P O Hebert and Senator John Slidell * * * To our mind, Governor Hebert is preferable to Senator Slidell   His antecedents are better, his political character less clouded, his personal honor is undoubted, his services to the state of his birth have not been small, he has served his country abroad with credit and honor, and at home, as well as abroad, has ever borne the character of an honorable, high-toned gentleman—' without fear and above reproach.' "

Governor Hebert's name was strongly urged by his party in Louisiana for a cabinet place, as secretary of war, under both Pierce and Buchanan   In a letter to the " Daily Delta," New Orleans, February 7, 1853, is the following, under the heading "The New Cabinet—Colonel Hebert "·   " In your weekly edition of the 30th ultimo I read an interesting and vigorous article on the subject of the cabinet of General Pierce, wherein the name of our new governor, P. O Hebert, was powerfully urged as a proper man to fill the secretaryship of war "   In the "Daily Delta " of December 10, 1856, is the following "Since the Democratic triumph, the press, generally, appears to be actively engaged in speculating upon the composition of the next cabinet. * * * I know of no one better calculated to fill the office, or more deserving of the honor, than Governor P. O Hebert   His thorough military education, together with his practical knowledge of his profession, his profound knowledge of the political history of the country, and his adaptability to the exigencies of the times, added to the distinguished position he has already occupied in his native state, can not fail to place his name high on the list of those spoken of for cabinet appointments   The governor, moreover, has strong claims upon his party * * * Not only did his own state reap the benefit of his labors and influence, but he extended his mission to the North   New York received him with all the honors due to his past services, and applauded his patriotic sentiments and true democratic spirit "

Hebert was governor of Louisiana from January 1, 1853, to January 28, 1856, one of his chief appointments during his administration being that of his former West Point classmate, W T Sherman, as president of the Louisiana Military Academy, at Alexandria

On December 12, 1860, ex-Governor Hebert received his commission from Governor Thomas Overton Moore as "member of the Military Board of Louisiana," and he was the first field officer commissioned by Governor Moore, in behalf of the "Independent State of Louisiana." In the early part of 1861, the Hon Jefferson Davis, appointed Governor Hebert one of the five brigadier-generals of the provisional army. This was before the Confederate army was organized. The other four, were Generals Robert E. Lee, Beauregard, Albert Sidney Johnston and John B Magruder. All were subsequently appointed brigadier generals in the Confederate army, Governor Hebert being placed in command of Louisiana, and afterwards given command of the Trans-Mississippi department, where he remained until relieved by General Magruder, Governor Hebert being ordered to the command of the department of Texas. General Kirby Smith subsequently relieved General Magruder, and the latter assumed command of the department of Texas, Governor Hebert being transferred to the command of the defenses of Galveston. General Hebert subsequently was in command of the subdistrict of North Louisiana, and was in the battle at Milliken s Bend, La

The following extract is from an article in a North Louisiana paper of that day, headed, "General Hebert and the Defences of North Louisiana." "It was fortunate for us that the immediate direction and control of military affairs in our region at such a time, fell into the hands of so skillful and energetic a commander as the gallant soldier whose name heads this article. He had in his district but two battalions of cavalry and a few light guns to resist the advances and raids of a force exceeding a hundred thousand men, the flower of the Federal army, and the formidable assault of the enemy's gun-boats. Instead of withdrawing to Red river, he waived the fearful odds and addressed himself energetically to the defense of his district. He infused his own energy and spirit into the troops, and the battalions accomplished wonders in checking the inroads of the vast army sweeping along our border, and Fort Beauregard, under his stirring order to hold it until the last man fell, successfully drove back the gun-boats. To-day, instead of presenting the gloomy spectacle of wasted and abandoned farms our country is smiling in peace and security, with the prospect of abundant crops to brighten and bless the land. To General Hebert, as the chief instrumentality, are we indebted for this, and to him is due the thanks of every man, woman and child in the district; more than this, we understand that General Hebert, several weeks since, had determined on a plan of attack which would seriously have crippled Grant's army, by breaking up his line of transportation and cutting off his supplies. It seems remarkable that that line should have been kept up for weeks, with but a comparatively small escort of troops, passing down the whole line of Madison, when there were forces in striking distance, that could have broken it up, supplying Grant's whole army while it was encircling Vicksburg, with its vast masses of troops. Had General Hebert's views in regard to these movements been adopted, this would

not have been the case, a powerful co-operative movement in favor of Vicksburg would doubtless have been established, and Grant by this would have
inevitably been driven back   We fear it is now too late to inflict on the enemy
the damage which the late opportunity presented, but we hope for the best ''
    In this connection the following letter explains itself

"HEADQUARTERS, SUBDISTRICT NORTH LOUISIANA,
"VIENNA, LA , Nov 25, 1863
"Major E Surget, Assistant Adjutant-General, Alexandria, La ·

    "MAJOR   I would respectfully call the attention of the major-general com-
manding to that portion of the letter of instructions, from department headquarters, requiring Colonel Harrison, a subordinate officer under my command,
to report direct to district headquarters.   *This*, it is true, is corrected in the
endorsement at district headquarters, by command of the major-general commanding   As the order originally stood, however, I was deprived entirely of
my command, small as it is   There certainly must have been some motive for
this   It is but simple justice to me that I should have been informed of the
reason   If I have in any manner neglected my duty I am clearly liable to
charges   The command of this subdistrict never has been a very desirable one—
still less so now   The major general commanding, no doubt, remembers how often
I have applied, both in writing and verbally, to be relieved from it and assigned
to a better one   This is naturally a subject of painful reflection to me, conscious
as I am of having performed my duty faithfully and of having done all that
could be done under the adverse circumstances which have surrounded me,
since I have been in command of the subdistrict   These, it is not now my purpose
to enumerate or dwell upon, but simply to recall the fact to the major-general
commanding   It is little to say that I was, at the very first, sorely disap-
pointed in the object for which I sought this command, from the want of a
proper force, which had been promised me   The records of the department will
show how I pointed out and how anxious I was to attempt the relief of
Vicksburg by striking a fatal blow upon the long and scattered columns of
General Grant on this side of the river, on his march to invest that city from
below   For *then* it was manifest that the true defense of Vicksburg was on
this side.   This my acts, the records of my office, and the military history of
the subdistrict will show   that if I have accomplished little or nothing, it was not
from want of zeal or capacity or owing to the absence of knowledge of what
should and *could* have been accomplished had the military means been at my dis-
posal   It may have been my *misfortune*, not my *fault*, that I have been so
placed   The necessities of the service, the invasion of the enemy in different
columns, the few troops disposable in the department—all, no doubt, combined—
prevented my having the force I so much desired, and which the defense of and
operations in this section of the country so eminently required   I trust that the
major-general commanding will not, for a moment suppose that I write in a

spirit of fault-finding or with a desire to repine unnecessarily at my lot—well knowing that in military as well as in other positions *opportunity*, or the want of it, frequently fixes the fame or obscurity of the officer. I am, perhaps, also not in too humble a position to escape misrepresentation and calumny: To be eliminated irregularly from a service and a cause which I have entered with my heart and soul, and in which I have at stake my life, fortune and honor, and that of all those I hold most dear, to be "overslaughed" without apparent cause, to be condemned without a hearing, or allowed the poor boon of the right of vindication, is, it will be conceded, hardly fair to myself personally or officially, to say nothing of military justice and the recognized regulations and usages of the service. In a former war, I acquired an honorable, although, perhaps, humble reputation. I wish to retain it in this, and leave *that*, if nothing else, to my children

"I have the honor to be, your obedient servant,

"P. O. Hebert,
"Brig.-Gen'l Comdg., P. A. C. S.

"Official: Jesse W. Sparks,
"Lieutenant and A. D. C."

The following is from a Texas paper and is dated "Camp Parsons," February 1, 1861. "Yesterday, the 31st ultimo, General Hebert came down attended by Adjutant Davis and Major Dennis, to review the 'gallant Fourth.' * * * The general and staff dined with the colonel at the encampment * * * He endeared himself to officers and men by his free and easy manners, social qualities and good 'wagon-horse sense' (I don't know any better way to express it). I can qualify it by saying that the ideas he advanced relative to the great struggle in which we are engaged, show thought and patient investigation. And to the friends of Parsons' regiment, and they are many, I will give a brief sketch of our general. I should suppose him to be about forty-five years old, about five feet ten inches high, finely formed, well proportioned and erect in carriage; black, wavy hair, with occasional streaks of gray, heavy moustache, almost white, a laughing blue eye, fine head, etc., and, so far from the hauteur and aristocratic proclivities of which he was accused, I imagine him to be a boon companion among friends in private circles. He is a native of Louisiana, graduated at West Point. * * * Texas can not boast a more graceful rider than he. Upon the whole, he is the right man in the right place. The general seemed well pleased with his trip, and says he will visit us again soon. The men of the regiment were highly pleased with him, which they attested by 'three cheers for General Hebert,' as he left the camps, which was responded to with a vim."

A Houston, Texas, paper of 1861, says: "General Hebert's call on our people to be ready to resist an invasion by our seacoast, will go through the land like a trumpet blast. His directions for preparation are clear, simple

and feasible, and if attended to as they undoubtedly will be, will place ten
thousand well armed men at his command in a week."

A Shreveport, La., paper of February 18, 1862, says   "Ex-Governor
Hebert, now a general in the Confederate service, arrived in our vicinity last
week with a small suite and pitched his marquee near Mr. Joe Howell's Springs
Unlike many officers who have preceded him, General Hebert has not made the
least gorgeous display, but quietly settled down with his military family in a
park   Notwithstanding that we have always differed with General Hebert in
politics, we cheerfully admit that he is a perfect model of a real Creole gentleman."

"At the close of the war, General E Kirby Smith turned over
his command of the Trans-Mississippi department to General Magruder, who
in his turn, transferred the command to General Hebert, Generals Smith and
Magruder intending to leave that night for Mexico   The next day General
Hebert surrendered to General Gordon Granger, who desired him to keep his
sword and courteously sent him and his family by special transport to New
Orleans   In July, 1865, Governor Hebert made application to have his dis-
abilities removed under the proclamation of President Johnson   The application was referred to General Sherman, then at St Louis, indorsed by him,
sent to General Thomas' headquarters at Louisville, forwarded to Washington,
and approved a few hours after arrival by the President   During the Grant
and Greely campaign, Governor Hebert was the leader in this state (Louisiana),
in the interests of the latter and was the author of the popular motto. 'All
roads from Greely lead to Grant' Notwithstanding that Governor Hebert was
such a persistent opponent, President Grant requested Governor Kellogg to
appoint Governor Hebert a member of the 'Board of State Engineers' In
1873 President Grant appointed Governor Hebert one of the Commissioners
of Engineers for the Mississippi Levees, Generals Abbott and Warren and
Major Benyard comprising the military, and Governor Hebert and Colonel
Sickles, of Arkansas, the civil, engineers ' [The above is an extract from an
obituary on Governor Hebert]

During Grant's administration Governor Hebert and Colonel Forshey
advocated the Fort St Philip canal, to prevent overflows of the Mississippi
river, in opposition to the jetty system of Captain Eads

The "Daily States," New Orleans, August 30, 1880, says   "Louisiana
mourns the death of one of her noblest and truest sons   It is a painful duty to
announce the death of ex-Governor Hebert   In the war he was assigned to an
important command, and, although not brought actively into service in the field,
yet his military education and experience made him a valuable and efficient
commander"

For nearly twenty-five years Governor Hebert was president of the
"Metaire Jockey Club," and took an active interest in sporting matters up
to the hour of his death   In Louisiana Biographies," by A Meynier, Jr,

we find the following in regard to " Paul O Hebert, twelfth Governor of
Louisiana " " Governor Hebert, for several years prior to the war, and two
years after it, was president of the jockey club of New Orleans He was a
' bon vivant and very fond of society, which his sociability attracted, and his
ample means, prior to the war, enabled him to enjoy He was well known as
an elegant writer and speaker, and the productions of his pen were noted for
their brilliancy and beautiful expression "

Governor Hebert was also a lover of art, and a connoisseur and collector
of fine pictures, glass and china He was the owner of one of the finest pieces
of statuary in Louisiana at that day—a life-sized statue of the " Christian
Martyr," by Giovanni Ardenti—which the Governor bought of the artist at
Milan, Italy, in one of his travels abroad

General Grant was a warm personal friend of Governor Hebert Their
friendship began at West Point and lasted for the rest of their lives (Hebert is
mentioned in Grant's Memoirs), and, while President, Grant showed his old
friend all the favors in his power, and he was often the guest of the White
House It was Grant's wish to appoint Hebert minister to Belgium The
following item appeared in the " New Orleans Times," June 26, 1875 · " Information has been received here that J Russell Jones, our minister resident at
Brussels, contemplates resigning at an early date. (Washington special to
Cincinnati Gazette) Last winter, when Mr Jones' retirement was contem-
plated, the President told Mr. Fisk that when the vacancy in the Belgian
ministry occurred he should tender the position to Governor P O Hebert, of
this state As the President is not given to changing his mind, it is probable
that Governor Hebert will be nominated "

In an account of a political banquet, the " National Republican," Washington, March 19 1874 has the following mention of Governor Hebert "At
the table, quietly sipping his claret, with his gray mustache waxed and pointed
à la Napoleon III , is the courtly ex governor of Louisiana, General Paul O
Hebert, whose achievements in the fields of politics and war are no less brilliant
than his triumphs in the fashionable salon." " Before the close of the war
Governor Hebert was raised to the rank of major-general, though his commission was never signed by President Davis In a letter to Mrs Saunders,
Ben LaBree, author of " The Confederate Soldier in the Civil War," says · " I
think General Paul O Hebert was a major-general by appointment of the
governor of Louisiana, and he was also a major general by virtue of his command under the Confederate government , and I believe there were commissions made out for General Hebert and quite a number of others to take the
rank of major-general, but they were never signed by President Davis There
are a couple of generals who were given the title of lieutenant-general, but
their commissions had never been signed; their rank, however, has never
been disputed, and this is the same in General P. O Hebert s case " In another
letter from Mr LaBree dated April 18 1898 he says "General Hebert's

grade was certainly that of major-general   He commanded a department of the
Confederacy, and that alone gave him the rank of major-general "   Brigadier-
General Louis Hebert, first cousin and contemporary of General P O Hebert,
corroborates Mr. LaBree's statement as to P. O Hebert being a major-
general   Governor Hebert was a charter member of the "Aztec Club,"
founded by the officers of the victorious American army in the City of Mexico in
1848   When governor of Louisiana, in 1856, in his last message to the legislature Governor Hebert says " The wild spirit of fanaticism, which has for
many years disturbed the repose of the country, has steadily increased in
power and influence   It controls the councils of several states, nullifies the
laws of Congress enacted for the protection of our property, and resists the
execution of them, even to the shedding of blood,   It has grown so powerful
that it now aspires to control the Federal legislature   The fact can no longer
be concealed, however much it may be regretted. The slave-holding states are
warned in time , they should be prepared for the issue   If it must come, the
sooner the better   The time for concessions on our part and compromises has
passed   If the Union can not be maintained upon the just and wholesome
principles of the Constitution, concessions and compromises will only retard its
dissolution, not save it   They have had, thus far, no other result than to en-
courage attack and to increase the number of Abolitionists   It would, however, be premature to suggest practical measures of resistance or retaliation
The present session of Congress will develop fully the plans of that party
Your own action must depend, in a great measure, upon the course which they
shall pursue   The responsibility will be upon those who have forced us, in
defense of our most sacred rights, of our honor, and of our very existence to
resort to extreme remedies "

    Governor Hebert died in New Orleans August 29, 1880, and is buried at
St Paul's church, Bayou Goula, Iberville, near his old plantation homestead.
His second wife survived him several years   The following obituary appeared
in the New Orleans " Picayune" on the death of Mrs. Hebert, October 18,
1893   "On the 18th instant, at 7 P M , died, at Atlanta, Ga , Mrs. Penelope
L Andrews Hebert, widow and second wife of the late Governor Paul O
Hebert, with whose name were associated many of the most honorable memories
of the state of Louisiana, which for four years Governor Hebert served as
governor, with great distinction   Mrs Hebert was married to Governor Hebert
in August, 1861, on the plantation of her father, Mr John Andrews, whose
plantation, ' Belle Grove,' in Iberville Parish, was one of the largest and finest
sugar estates in Louisiana, the splendid residence on the place being palatial in
all its appointments and fittings, and being famous for its elegance from Vicksburg to New Orleans   Mrs Hebert's youth was passed amid the scenes of
lavish and hospitable entertainment, for which Belle Grove was celebrated, both
before and after the war," etc

    After the death of Governor Hebert, Mrs Hebert continued her residence

VINCERE VEL MORI

McDowall

on the "Home Place," a magnificent plantation, situated about a mile back of Bayou Goula, in Iberville Parish, and which from before the beginning of this century has been the homestead of the Heberts

Mrs Hebert was a woman of remarkable qualities With the beauty and gentleness of a woman she united the courage and firmness of a man She followed her husband's command during the four years of war, living in camp and enduring the hardships of army life at that time

Governor Hebert by his second marriage had six children, viz Paul Hebert, born at Houston, Texas, May 11, 1862, died in camp at Vienna, La, October 3, 1863; Ignace Hebert, born and died in camp at Vienna, La, December, 1863; Marie Eugenie Hamilton Hebert, Paul Octave Hebert, Pauline Octavie Hebert, and Penelope Lynch Adams Andrews Hebert, born in Iberville, La The only surviving children of this family are Paul O Hebert and Pauline Octavie Hebert, the former is a civil engineer and a graduate of the Jesuit College, Spring Hill, Mobile, Ala, and of the Van Rensselaer Polytechnic, Troy, N Y He married his first cousin, Angela Lewis Morse Pauline Octavie Hebert, married George Boykin Saunders, of Atlanta, Ga, in August, 1893, whose father was Dr Simon Hardy Saunders, who married Victoria McCants Before the war Dr Saunders was a member of the Georgia legislature, and mayor of Griffin, Ga. During the war he was a surgeon, with the rank of major, in Doyle's regiment, the 53d of Georgia He was a son of John Saunders and Virginia Boykin, of Southampton county, Va The "immigrant ancestor" of the Saunders of Virginia, came from Monmouthshire, in the west of England, and was exiled for taking part in the "Monmouth Rebellion" He patented lands in Goochland county, Va., in 1690

Virginia Boykin Saunders was a daughter of Major Simon Boykin, of Southampton county, Va, who was a descendant of Edward Boykin, of Wales, who settled in the Isle of Wight county, Va, and patented a great deal of land there in 1685.

Mrs Simon H. Saunders, was a daughter of Dr Robert Pembroke McCants, of Alabama, and his wife Caroline Allen, a daughter of Judge George Allen, of Abbeville District, South Carolina, and his wife, Ruth Linton These Allens and Lintons were descendants of the Clark and Randolph families of Virginia.

" McDowall, McDougall, McDugall or McOul (Lord of Lorn), quarterly, first and fourth, arms Az a lion ramp or, second and third or a lymphad sa., with a beacon on the topmast ppr. Crest An arm in armour embowed fesseways, couped ppr. holding a cross crosslet fitchée Motto Vincam vel mori " Burke.

When Mrs. Elizabeth McDowell Welch was traveling in Europe she secured and brought home with her to the United States the arms above described, from the Herald's College, London, England, as the arms belonging to the M'Dowells of this country The motto differ from that above in that it has Vincere in place of Vincam

The McDowells of this country and the old have intermarried with the Irvines so often that the Irvine pedigrees would hardly be complete without a short sketch of the McDowells

"Of all the fierce and warlike septs that ranged themselves beside the Campbells, under the leadership of the chiefs of the name, in the struggles so replete with deeds of crime and heroism, of oppression and stubborn resistance, which had their fruit in the overthrow of the right line of the Stuarts, there was none more respectable, nor one which more perfectly illustrated the best qualities of their race than the sons of Dowall   Sprung from Dougall, the son of Ronald, the son of the great and famous Somerland, they had, from the misty ages, marched and fought under the cloudberry bush, as the badge of their clan, and had marshalled under the banner of the ancient Lords of Lorn, the chiefs of their race   The form of McDowell was adopted by those of the McDougal clan who held lands in Galloway, to which they, the Black Gaels, had given its name   The latter branch became allied by blood and intermarriages with the Campbells Presbyterians of the strictest sect, and, deeply imbued with the love of civil and religious freedom which has ever characterized the followers of John Knox, they found their natural leaders in the house of Argyle   In what degree related to the chiefs of the name was the McDowell who left behind him the hills of his native Argyleshire, to settle with others of his name and kindred and religion in the north of Ireland, during the protectorate of Cromwell, can not be accurately stated, he was, so far as can be gleaned from vague traditions, one of the most reputable of the colonists who there founded the race known as the 'Scotch Irish,' the characteristics of which have since been so splendidly attested by its heroes, scholars, orators, theologians and statesmen all over the world   This Scotch colonist, McDowell, had, among other children, a son Ephraim which of itself, indicates that he was a child of the covenant   It was fitting that Ephraim McDowell should become, at the age of sixteen years one of the Scotch-Irish Presbyterians who flew to the defense of heroic Londonderry on the approach of McDonald of Antrim, on the 9th of December, 1688, and that he should be one of the band who closed the gates against the native Irishry, intent on blood and rapine   During the long siege that followed, the memory of which will ever bid defiance to the effacing hand of time, and in which the devoted preacher, George Walker, and the brave Murray, at the head of their undisciplined fellow citizens—farmers, shopkeepers, mechanics and apprentices but Protestants and Presbyterians—successfully repelled the assaults of Rosen, Marmont, Persignan and Hamilton, the McDowell was conspicuous for endurance and bravery in a band where all were brave as the most heroic Greek who fell at Thermopylæ.

" The maiden name of the woman who became the worthy helpmeet of the Londonderry soldier boy was Margaret Irvine, his own full first cousin   She was a member of an honorable Scotch family who settled in Ireland at the same time as their kin people the McDowell   The name Irvin, Irvine,

Irving, Irwin and Erwin are identical—those bearing the name thus variously spelled being branches from the same tree   This name was, and is, one of note in Scotland, where those who bore it had intermarried with the most prominent families of the kingdom, breeding races of soldiers, statesmen, orators and divines "

Ephraim McDowell,

"Who fought at Boyne river   as well as at Londonderry, was already an elderly man when, with his two sons, John and James, his two daughters, Mary and Margaret, and numerous kinsmen and co-religionists, he immigrated to America to build for himself and his a new home   * * *   The exact date of his arrival in Pennsylvania is not known   Certain it is, that about 1729, Ephraim and his family, and numerous other McDowells, Irvines, Campbells, McElroys and Mitchells, came over and settled in the same Pennsylvania county   T M GREEN

The strong traits of character that marked the personality of the first McDowells and Irvines, distinguishes them still, and the love of warfare, that seems to lie at the very root of their nature, has made their names famous in all the wars of this country

Major Henry Clay McDowell.

Prominent among the distinguished McDowells of Kentucky, and of the United States, is Major Henry C McDowell of Lexington, Ky

Major McDowell is a direct descendant of John Irvine, the immigrant, who came to this country together with the seven Irvine brothers who arrived in this country in 1729   Ephraim McDowell, who married his cousin, Margaret Irvine, and who fought at Boyne River, or " Boyne Water," as the Irish say, and at Londonderry, came to America with the Campbells, McElroys, Mitchells and Irvines, all related to one another

Abram Irvine was the son of John Irvine, the immigrant   The daughter of Abram Irvine and Mary Dean, Anna, married Samuel McDowell   Major Henry C McDowell is a grandson of Samuel McDowell and Anna Irvine   I copy a short notice of Major McDowell which appeared in a volume of " Kentucky Biographies

"Henry Clay McDowell, son of William Adair McDowell and Maria Hawkins Harvey, born in Fincastle county, Virginia, in 1832, coming to Kentucky in 1830, when his father returned to his native State   He graduated at

8

the Louisville Law School, and won his way to a successful practice in his
profession, being for some years a partner of his brother-in-law, Judge Bland
Ballard   He was among the earliest in Kentucky to take up arms for the
Union on breaking out of the Civil War, and was commissioned by Mr
Lincoln as assistant Adjutant General, and served on the staff of Gen Rous-
seau and Gen Boyle   He was afterwards commissioned by Mr Lincoln as
United States Marshal for Kentucky, being the same office held by his grand-
father, Samuel McDowell, under commission of General Washington

"He married Anna Clay, daughter of Lieutenant-Colonel Henry Clay,
who was killed at the battle of Buena Vista, and was a son of the matchless
orator, Henry Clay

" Major McDowell purchased Ashland, the home of his wife's grandfather, and lives at ease, devoting himself to agricultural pursuits, and giving
some attention to the Lexington & Eastern Railway Companies, of which he
is president   In politics he was first a Whig, later a Republican

" Major McDowell appears yet in his prime   The time to do him justice
is far distant, it is to be hoped, as no man's history can be rightly written until
his biographer may look from the beginning of his life to its close "

Another descendant of the same line as Major H. C McDowell, was the
late Judge Alexander Keith Marshall McDowell, who lies buried at Cynthiana, Ky   He was born in Mercer county, Kentucky, in 1806   He was a
soldier in the Black Hawk War and a soldier in the Confederate army in time of
the late Civil War   Judge McDowell was as near perfect manhood as a human
being could be   He was a scholar, a soldier and a true Christian   At the time
of his death it was said of him   Judge McDowell has bequeathed to his
descendants a legacy of far more worth than the long line of ancestry from
which he came, or the armorial bearing that would have been carved above his
place of repose had he died in Scotland, the father of his people—a spotless
name   Carve above his tomb, Resurgam   He was a true Christian

—   . .

Major and Doctor Hervey McDowell.

Dr. Hervey McDowell is the son of Capt John Lyle McDowell and his
wife, Nancy Vance   Major McDowell combines in a remarkable degree the
traits of his family   About his manner there is a quiet reserve and a bearing
that impress thoughtful observers with a certain knowledge that he is a thorough'
gentleman, incapable of falsehood, without fear, and full of all the amenities of
life

He graduated, in 1856, at a military school at Frankfort, Ky , and later at
a celebrated medical college in St Louis, Mo.

He w -. in the late Civil War commissioned Major in the Confederate

Army, and fought from its beginning to the close with the most dauntless courage. So much for the man in whose veins runs the blood of Dougall, the son of Roland.

The Irvines, Irvins, Irvings, Ervines, Erwins of the Old Country and the New.

I place the Irvines, etc., of the old country, first, in order to prove the immutable law of hereditament. The germ of life in man is like the seed of the thistle that may be borne thousands of miles and fall into rich loam and it will come up a thistle, as all of its fathers were. It may be warped by strong winds, or increased in size by the rich nourishment of its new home, but it will still bear the unmistakable marks of its ancestors, and wounds if one handles it too roughly. The same courage and strength of mind that the ancestors of the Irvines of the old country displayed on many a battlefield have been repeated by their descendants in this new land. The same ability in literature, statesmanship and theology that characterized many an Irvine of the old country, have distinguished the Irvines of America.

The training and easy living of many generations of pure-blooded men make aristocrats. The ease that wealth and careful training of many generations of aristocrats give enervates and depletes them. They diminish in size and strength, and lose, in a measure, their hardihood and capacity to endure, but never lose the distinctive characteristics of their race.

Read the long list of honors won by the Irvines of Scotland, England and Ireland, and then follow their descendants from 1729, when they first landed in Pennsylvania, down to the present time, and be convinced that the law of hereditament in man is as immutable as the law that governs the animal and vegetable worlds. Is not the blood in man as strong to paint its likeness, from generation to generation, as the sap that colors the rose on its tree with unchanging fidelity from year to year and from age to age, in all climates and in every land?

Irvines of the Old Country.

I copy this passage from "The Scottish Nation," by William Anderson, page 537

"Irvine, a surname of ancient standing in Scotland, supposed to have been originally Erevine, the latter word derived by some antiquarians, from the Celtic-Scythic Erin vine or fein, that is a stout westland man; Erin west (the native name of Ireland; Iym wes of Scotia ... a strong,

resolute man Nisbet (System of Heraldry, Vol II , App p 69) says that when
the colonies of the Gauls came from the west coast of Spain and seated themselves on the east coasts of Erin and in the west hills and islands of Albyn, the
Erevincs came to both these islands. In the latter country they had their seat
in a part of Ayrshire, called Cunningham, and gave their name to the river and
their own place of residence, now the town of Irvine One of them, Crine
Erwine, was a thane of Dull, and seneschal and collector of all the King's rents
in the western isles   He married the Princess Beatrix, eldest daughter of
Malcolm II , and was father of Duncan I , King of Scotland   Some of this
family went to Dumfriesshire, and settled on the river Esk, where one of them
obtained, by marriage, the lands of Bonshaw, in that county   A descendant
of his, in the seventeenth century, rendered his name obnoxious by his cruel
persecutions of the Covenanters "

This passage confirms what Rev Dr Christopher Irvine, of Mountjoy
Omagh, Ireland, says in a recent letter to me about the Irvines. Rev Dr
Christopher Irvine wrote a history of the Irvines of Bonshaw Irish branch, which
has not been published   It was placed in the hands of a publisher for publica-
tion, but the publisher failed in business and the manuscript history was lost.
The following is the entire letter of Rev Dr Christopher Irvine

" The Irvines, Irvings, or Irwins, were one of the ancient original families,
or clans, of Dumfriesshire, Scotland   They were located in Annandale, Evis-
dale, Eskdale and Wanchopdale on the coast of this shire, close to the borders
of England   They developed into five separate divisions or sub-clans by the
year 1500, or the sixteenth century, and from the year 1600 became widely
spread through England and Ireland   Between 1610 and 1660, the chief exodus
to Ireland took place   Members of the different sub-clans settled in Ulster in the
northern counties of that province   The Irvings of Bonshaw were the first, or
chief sub-clans, and the Laird of Bonshaw was recognized as the chieftain of
the whole Dumfriesshire clan or name   King Robert Bruce made one of this
family, Sir William Irvine, his secretary, and gave him the Forest of Drum, in
Aberdeenshire, and thus were derived the various branches of the name in the
north of Scotland   The Irvines of Drum, the lineal descendants of Sir William,
still retain the possessions granted them by Robert Bruce

" The Irvines of Bonshaw suffered much in the wars with England, Bonshaw
having been several times taken and burned to the ground by the English
armies   Edward Irving, of Bonshaw (1566 to 1605), was a turbulent chieftain,
and carried on successful family feuds with rival clans — Maxwells, Kirkpatricks,
Bells, etc , for which he was outlawed by the Scottish government   He survived the government outlawries and confiscations, and strengthened himself by
alliances with the Johnstons, the most powerful of the Dumfriesshire clans, his
son Christopher having married Margaret, the daughter of Johnston, chieftain
of that clan   By this alliance the Johnstons and Irvines, with their allies, were
able to defeat the Lord Warden at the head of the government troops at the

battle of Dryfersands, 1593, so that the King had to make peace with them, and appoint Johnston his head warden   The descendants of this Christopher Irving continued to reside at Bonshaw, and the present owner, Colonel John Beaufin Irving, is the lineal heir   Among his predecessors who were distinguished as officers in the army was Sir Paulus Aemilius Irving, Baronet   The next brother of Edward of Bonshaw was Christopher of Robgilland Annan, known by the border name of Black Christie   He was also a turbulent chief, engaged in the cause of Queen Mary, 1567, etc   His son, John, married Mary, daughter of Johnston, of Newbie, and then son, Christopher, settled in County Fermanagh, Ireland, in 1613   From him are descended the Irvines, or Irvings, of Fermanagh, represented by Captain William D'Arcy Irvine of Castle Irvine   One of the sons of Christopher Irvine, Sir Gerard Irvine, Baronet, was greatly distinguished in the Irish Rebellion of 1641   He was an officer in the Royal Army and fought on the side of the King against the Roundheads, both in Ireland and Scotland   He was also engaged on the side of King William III in the wars of 1689, and died that year in Duke Schomberg's camp in Dundalk   Colonel William Irvine, of Castle Irvine, presided over the great meeting of volunteers at Dungannon in 1782   The several younger branches of the family included the Irvines of Killadees, Greenhill, St. Aidens, etc   Though it may be hard to trace the several families of Irvines who settled in Ireland, yet they mostly all belonged to the Dumfriesshire clan, though some may have come from Aberdeen and the north of Scotland "

Col William Irvine, of Castle Irvine born July 15, 1734, member for Ratoath in the Irish House of Commons, was High Sheriff County Fermanagh 1758 and of Tyrone 1768. He married, first, December 10, 1755, Hon Flora Caroline Cole, daughter of John, first Lord Mount Florence, she died October 20, 1757, leaving a son, Christopher, died young   He married, second, February 23, 1760, Sophia, daughter of Gorges Lowther, Esq . of Kilrue, County Meath (by Judith his wife, daughter of John Usher and Mary his wife, only daughter of George, first Lord St George), and had eight sons and eight daughters

    I. GEORGE MARCUS, of whom presently

    II WILLIAM HENRY, Rector of Tara and Dunshaughlin, County Meath, Justice of Peace for that county, born 1763, married Elizabeth, daughter of James Hamilton, Esq , of Sheephill, County Dublin, and died 1839, leaving by her (who died April 26, 1859,) issue

        1 Gorges Lowther, Rector of Rathregan, County Meath, married December, 1827, Henrietta Florence, daughter of Christopher Edmund John Nugent, Esq , of Bobsgrove, and by her (who died March, 1834,) had two daughters, Sophia, married John G Holmes, Esq , of Rockwood, County Galway, and Henrietta, married Clement Hammerton, Esq , M. D   Rev G Irvine died November, 1838

2 James, Commander, Royal Navy, of Hardwick Place, Dublin, died unmarried, November, 1867

3 Henry, of Rosslare, County Wexford, and Kilmore, County Tyrone, born 1802, married 1829, Elizabeth, daughter of Ebenezer Radford Rowe, Esq, of Ballyharty, County Wexford, and twin sister of Sophia, wife of Sir Thomas Esmonde, Bart, and has issue, John William Henry, born 1831, William Henry, late Captain Third Regiment (Buffs), married Maria Jane, daughter of Arthur Edward Knox, Esq, of Castlerea, by Lady Jane Parsons his wife, daughter of Lawrence, second Earl of Rosse, and has a daughter, Edith

4 St George Caulfeild, Rector of Kilmessan, County Meath, married Georgina, daughter of Nathaniel Preston, Esq, of Swainstown, County Meath, and had a daughter, Georgina, married Surgeon-Major McNalty

5 Hans, M D, died unmarried

1. Charlotte, died unmarried, 1874

2 Harriet, died unmarried

3 Caroline, married Rev John Lowe, Rector of Dunshaughlin, County Meath

III CHRISTOPHER HENRY HAMILTON, Royal Navy, born 1776, died unmarried

IV GEORGE ST. GEORGE, Major in the army, of Ballinabown, County Wexford, High Sheriff, 1804, born 1771, married, first, Bridget, daughter of Maurice Howlin D'Arcy, Esq, of Cooline, County Wexford, she died without issue He married, second, Frances, daughter of Robert Doyne, Esq, of Wells, County Wexford, and had issue

1 Edward Tottenham, of St Aidans, County Wexford, Justice of the Peace and D L, High Sheriff, County Wexford 1861, late Captain Sixteenth Lancers, born 1832, married 1861, Elizabeth Beatrice, daughter of Edward Gonne Bell, Esq, of Streamstown, County Mayo, and has had issue, Edward St George Tottenham, born February 12, 1883, Mary Sophia Georgina, born February 13, 1863, died January 8, 1864

1 Frances Eleanor D'Arcy, married 1856, Rev. Charles Elrington

2 Sophia Maria, married, first, 1852, James Butler, Esq, of Castile Crine, second, 1860, Col I. H Graham, and died May 8, 1887.

V HENRY WILLIAM, born 1772, married Rebecca Cooke, and had an only daughter, Rebecca, married David Onge, Esq

VI AUDLEY MERVYN, born 1774, killed at Pondicherry

VII JOHN CAULFEILD, Captain in the army, Justice of the Peace County

Cork, born 1781, married Mary Broderick, daughter and co-heir of Henry Mitchell, Esq , of Mitchellsfort, County Cork, and relict of Grice Smyth, Esq , of Ballinattay, died without issue, 1850.

VIII HUGH LOWTHER, born 1783, killed at Monte Video

I SOPHIA MARIA, wife of Captain Carew Smith

II ELINOR JANE, wife of Henry Gonne Bell, Esq

III FLORENCE ELIZABETH ANN, wife of William Rathborne, Esq

IV OLIVIA EMILY, wife of George Lennox Conyngham, Esq

V FRANCES MARY, wife of Jones Irwin, Esq , of County Sligo

VI HARRIET, married John Carleton, Esq , of Mohill, County Leitrim

VII LETITIA ST PATRICIA MERVYN, wife of Colonel Alexander Stuart, only son of General James Stuart

VIII ELIZABETH EMILY, wife first of Ebenezer Radford Rowe, Esq , of Ballyharty, County Wexford, and second, of Samuel Green, Esq.

Col. Irvine died May, 1814 His eldest son, Major Gorges Marcus Irvine, of Castle Irvine, born November 26, 1760, married March 31, 1788, Elizabeth, daughter and heir of Judge D Arcy, Esq , of Dunmow Castle, County Meath (by Elizabeth his wife, daughter and heir of Richard Nugent, Esq , of Robbinstown)   (The D'Arcys of Dunmow, of whom Mr D'Arcy-Irvine is the heir general, were descended from the baronial house of D'Arcy, afterwards Earls of Holderness) By the heiress of D'Arcy (who died 1829) Major Irvine had four sons and five daughters

I WILLIAM D'ARCY, of whom hereafter

II RICHARD, E I Co , born 1794, died without issue

III GORGES MERVYN (Rev), born 1798

IV ST GEORGE, born 1801, married Miss Catherine Fennell.

V SOMERSET, R N , born 1809, married a daughter of Abraham Hargrave, Esq , of Cove, County Cork , died without issue 1850

I LOUISA, born 1791

II ELIZABETH, born 1795 , married Marquis Fernando Incontri, of Florence.

III SUSANNA AMELIA, born 1797, died unmarried 1870

IV SOPHIA, born 1799, married Arthur, Viscount Dungannon, and died March 21, 1880

V LETITIA, born 1805, died unmarried April 5, 1884, aged 78

Major Irvine died November 28, 1847, and was succeeded by his eldest son.

William D'Arcy Irvine, of Castle Irvine, born January 22, 1793, adopted the surname of D'Arcy. He married in 1817, Maria, daughter of Sir Henry Crooke, first baronet of Cole Brooke, County Fermanagh, and by her (who died July 18, 1838) had issue

I HENRY MERVYN D'ARCY IRVINE, his heir

II RICHARD D'ARCY, Treasurer of County Fermanagh, died unmarried 1857

III   WILLIAM D'ARCY, heir to his nephew
IV   FRANCIS D'ARCY, Major H M Indian Army, married 1854, Margaret,
      daughter of Col Sewell, and has issue, William, Robert Judge, Somerset,
      Maria Elizabeth and Henrietta
  V   ARTHUR D'ARCY, Captain in the Fermanagh Militia
VI   JOHN D'ARCY, Captain R N, died 1885
   I ELIZABETH, wife of John Caldwell Bloomfield, Esq, of Castle Cald-
      well, County Fermanagh
  II MARIA
      Mr Irvine died June 23, 1857, and was succeeded by his eldest son.

      Henry Mervyn D'Arcy Irvine, Esq, of Castle Irvine, High Sheriff County
Tyrone 1851, who by royal license, April 27, 1861, assumed the additional
surnames and arms of Mervyn and D'Arcy   He married October 16, 1862,
Huntly Mary, eldest daughter of Hon Francis Prittie, and by her (who died
March 2, 1864) left at his decease, July, 1870, a son—
      HENRY HUNTLY D ARCY IRVINE, Esq, of Castle Irvine, born
August 14, 1863 died unmarried January 9, 1882, and was succeeded by
his uncle, William D'Arcy Irvine, now of Castle Irvine

      Arms—Quarterly First and fourth arg a fess gu between three holly-
leaves vert, for Irvine, second, az. semée of cross-crosslets and three cinque-
foils arg, for D'Arcy, Third, or, a chevron sa, for Mervyn   Crests—First,
Irvine A gauntlet fessways issuant out of a cloud and holding a thistle all ppr,
Second, D Arcy On a chapeau gu turned up erm a bull passant sa, armed
or, Third, A squirrel sejant ppr cracking a nut gu   Motto—First, Irvine ·
Dum memor ipse mei, Second, D'Arcy Un Dieu, un roy, Third, Mervyn,
De Dieu est tout.

      Seat . Castle Irvine, Irvinestown

Irvine of Castle Irvine.

      Irvine, William D'Arcy, Esq, of Castle Irvine, County Fermanagh, form-
erly Captain Sixty-seventh Regiment, Justice of Peace and D L, High
Sheriff 1885, born 1823, married 1858, Louisa, daughter of Captain Cock-
burn, R A, and has had issue
   I WILLIAM D'ARCY, Lieutenant Ninety-ninth Regiment, served in the
      Zulu War, and Captain Third Battalion Royal Inniskillen Fusileers, died
      unmarried September 25, 1879
  II CHARLES COCKBURN D'ARCY, Captain Third Battalion Inniskillen
      Fusileers, High Sheriff 1886, born 1863, married March 13, 1884,
      Fanny Kathleen, daughter of Lieutenant-Colonel Jesse Lloyd, of Bally-
      leck, County Monaghan, and has issue

1 Charles William, born 1885
2 Henry Cockburn, born 1886
1 Violet Kathleen, born 1888

LINEAGE—The Irvines of Castle Irvine are of very ancient Scottish ancestry   They are directly descended from the Irvings of Bonshaw, County Dumfries, the first of the name on record being Robert de Herewme, A D 1226 (see Irving of Bonshaw)

Christopher Irvine, a lawyer, bred at the Temple, London, was the first of the family who settled in Ireland, upon a grant, from King James VI. of Scotland and I of England, of lands in Fermanagh   He built Castle Irvine, which was burnt by the rebels in 1641   He lived till after the Restoration, and died in 1666, at an advanced age   He married his cousin, Blanche, daughter of Edward Irvine, Laird of Stapleton (see Irving of Bonshaw), and had issue

I CHRISTOPHER, M D, born 1618, Physician-General to the States of Scotland, Historiographer to King Charles II, married Margaret, daughter of James Wishart, Laird of Pittarow, second son of Sir James Wishart and Lady Jean Douglas, third daughter of William, ninth Earl of Angus, and died 1693, leaving issue

    1 Christopher, M D, of Castle Irvine, born about 1642, succeeding to the Castle Irvine estates on the death of his uncle, Sir Gerard   He was High Sheriff County Fermanagh 1690, and Member of Parliament for the county from 1703 to 1713, married Phœbe, daughter of Sir George Hume, Baronet, of Castle of Hume, and widow of Henry Blennerhassett, of Cavendish Castle, and died without issue May 9, 1714   She died 1710

    2 James, Surgeon-General, of Dumfries, married Miss Maxwell, and had one son, Christopher, who died young

    3 Thomas, married Sydney, daughter of Lancelot Carleton, of Rossfad, and died without issue 1694

    4 John, died unmarried, about 1698

II GERARD (Sir) of Ardscragh, County Tyrone, Lieutenant-Colonel in King Charles II's service before his Restoration, created a Baronet July 31, 1677, died at Dundalk Camp 1689, a Lieutenant Colonel in the Earl of Granard's regiment in King William's service, married, first, Catherine, daughter of Adam Cathcart, of Bandoragh, Scotland, and of Drumslager, County Tyrone (she died without issue), second, Mary, daughter of Major William Hamilton, and by her (who died 1685) had issue

    1 Christopher, born 1654, married Deborah, daughter and co-heiress of Henry Blennerhassett, Esq., of Castle Hassett, County Fermanagh, and died 1680 ? p s. p

    2 Charles, Lieutenant of horse, died unmarried 1684

    3 Gerard, drowned at Enniskillen School

    1 Margaret wife of John Crichton ancestor of the Earls Erne

9

    III LANCELOT, died unmarried

    IV WILLIAM

      I MARGARET, married, first, Colonel Richard Bell, County Dumfries, and had issue, second, Captain Thomas Maxwell, and third, David Rhynd, of Derryvullen, County Fermanagh

      II MARION, married, first, Andrew Johnston, second son of James Johnston, Laird of Beirholme, County Dumfries, second, her cousin, Lancelot Carleton, of Rossfad, and had issue, and third, Captain John Somerville

The third son William Irvine, of Ballindulla, was a Lieutenant of horse under King Charles II at the Battle of Worcester, where he was wounded, and High Sheriff for County Fermanagh 1681 He married, first, Elizabeth, daughter of Herbert Gledstanes, a Colonel under Gustavus Adolphus, King of Sweden and Governor of Walgast, and had issue

    I CHRISTOPHER, of whom afterwards

    II JOHN, ancestor of the Irvines of Killadeas (see Irvine of Killadeas)

    III CHARLES, Lieutenant-Colonel, married March 8, 1698, Margaret King, sister of William King, D D., Archbishop of Dublin, and died without issue 1745

    IV LANCELOT, Lieutenant in Brigadier Wolseley's Regiment of Inniskillen Horse, died unmarried 1701.

      I ELIZABETH, married, first, Samuel Eccles, Esq, and second, —— Mayne, County Fermanagh

      II MARGARET, married William Humphreys, Esq, of Dromard, who was attainted by James II in 1689

      III MARY, married James Johnston, Esq, High Sheriff, County Fermanagh, 1707

      IV KATHERINE, married Merrick Meige, Esq of Greenhill, County Fermanagh

      V MAGDALENE, married Robert Johnston, Esq.

Mr Irvine married secondly, Anne Armstrong, and by her had further issue

      V GERARD Capt, of Greenhill, married Alice Forster, and died without issue March 21, 1755

      VI REBECCA, died young

The eldest son, Christopher Irvine, commonly called Colonel Irvine, succeeded (on the fail of issue male of his uncles, Dr Irvine and Sir Gerard Irvine) to the Castle Irvine estates, in 1714, and was High Sheriff, County Fermanagh 1716 He died 1723, having married first, 1683, Mary, daughter of Rev Dr Bernard, and by her had two daughters, Mary (Mrs Hamilton), and Elizabeth, and secondly, 1693, Dorothy Anne, daughter of Jeffry Brett, by whom he left at his decease —

    I CHRISTOPHER

II CHARLES, married first, Susan Ferguson, by whom he had John, died unmarried, and Elizabeth, Mrs Humphreys, secondly, Anne Irvine, by whom he had John, and thirdly, Elizabeth Grant, who died without issue

The elder son, Christopher Irvine, Esq of Castle Irvine, High Sheriff for Fermanagh 1725, born April 15, 1697, married 1718, first, Dorcas, daughter of Col Alexander Montgomery, but by her had no issue He married, secondly, 1727, Elinor, daughter and ultimately co-heir of Audley Mervyn Esq of Trillick, County Tyrone (by Hon Olivia Coote, daughter of Richard, first Lord Colloony) and by her (who died July, 1767) had issue

   I WILLIAM, his heir
   II HENRY married 1759, Harriett, daughter of Benjamin Bunbury, Esq , of Kilfeacle, and had a daughter Mary, married Col John Caulfeild, of Donamon
   I OLIVIA, died unmarried.
   II MARY, died unmarried
   III ELIZABETH, died unmarried
   IV ELINOR, married June, 1766, Oliver Nugent, Esq , of Farrenconnel
  Mr Irvine died 1755 The elder son

(

9 781015 530966